THE BYTES BEHIND BLOCKS

THE BYTES BEHIND BLOCKS

AN ARCHITECT'S GUIDE TO BLOCKCHAIN

Nelson Petracek

Foreword by Miguel Torres

The Bytes Behind Blocks

An Architect's Guide to Blockchain

ISBN 978-1-5445-3382-7 Paperback

978-1-5445-3383-4 Ebook

CONTENTS

ACKNOWLEDGMENTS

Nicole Sanchez and Erin Moeller for their invaluable support and management of the entire process while I tried to weave this work into my schedule.

Brian Douglass, Barb MacLean, and Jim St. Clair for taking the time to review early drafts of the book and share their thoughts on its content. Their expertise and feedback are always appreciated!

Ann Scheuerell, Josipa Caran Safradin, and the entire TIBCO creative team for reviewing the content and providing valuable input. I'm sure they know more about blockchain than they ever wanted!

The awesome OOCTO & TIBCO LABS organization, and the whole team at TIBCO for all of their support.

Thanks to all!

FOREWORD

—Miguel Torres

Director of the Americas, Office of the CTO, TIBCO Software

Back in 2015, after my third or fourth reading of the Satoshi Nakamoto whitepaper,[1] I finally started to understand. Even though I could not yet imagine the implications of Bitcoin's invention, I could sense it had the potential of being pivotal for the digital world.

Shortly after that, I met Nelson. It took only one conversation to recognize that he profoundly understood not only blockchain concepts, but its game-changing benefits for the individual, the enterprise, and the economy as a whole.

Before long, Nelson and I were going all over California meeting with crypto startups and learning about their challenges. It didn't matter how complex or abstract the issue, Nelson could understand the principles, find innovative and creative solutions, and elegantly project them into new frontiers, all while explaining

---

[1] The name used by the presumed pseudonymous person or persons who developed Bitcoin, authored the Bitcoin whitepaper, and created and deployed Bitcoin's original reference implementation.

complex concepts to anyone. After more than six years working with Nelson, I have witnessed the same impressive skill applied to any technology. In short, Nelson is a 360-degree technologist who is deeply knowledgeable and passionate about his subject.

Once the new frontier, personal computers transformed the way we learn, work, socialize, and interact. Now, AI/ML, robotics, space exploration, and applied quantum physics have the potential to shift paradigms and transform what and how we do things. I believe blockchain and Web3 deserve a spot among these technologies. Once their full potential has been met, they will empower humans to do new things, or the same old things smarter and better.

However, all these innovations are tremendously complex. They require learning new terminology, syntax, and contextual and background specifics, as well as understanding the trade-offs the technology provides for a given situation. This is the main reason why *The Bytes Behind the Blocks* is so important. While addressing both neophyte and knowledgeable readers, it takes us on a journey through the most crucial blockchain and Web3 topics, and does so masterfully, explaining real-world problems and the possible solutions this new technology could offer.

Blockchain is one of those horizontal technologies that will inevitably affect almost every business vertical and intersect some of the toughest decisions yet to be made. From a career development viewpoint, it is becoming essential to understand primitive blockchain concepts and what they can bring to the technology toolbox for solving real-world challenges.

As digital properties start to trickle through our everyday actions (social media, banking, art, music, games, etc.), knowledge of the enabling technology and its risks and benefits is becoming crucial.

Starting with Web1, static web pages and emails were the killer apps of the internet as we know it. Everything was open. New markets and business models were born, and centralized companies like Google found a way to link everything and become Web1 winners and eventual gatekeepers.

Web2 saw the concentration of users into subnetworks within the internet where user-generated content was found, shared, and commented on. Facebook and Twitter came out on top.

Web3 changes Web1 and Web2 paradigms in which data ownership and identity are owned by centralized winners. By giving data value and control back to users, Web3 tokens and financial incentives become part of the security blueprint. Driven by the innovative concepts of digital scarcity, digital private property, user network ownership, and governance, Web3 opens the door to brand new business models.

Web3 is also almost all built on open-source code. Revenue isn't generated from selling software, but network use and usefulness create value. Composability has an exponential compound effect that helps these networks thrive and grow.

This book provides a clear and concise deep dive into the building blocks of the Web3 frontier and blockchain. It starts with why a blockchain is important or relevant, and in the process explains decentralized and permissionless networks, smart contracts, consensus algorithms, cryptography primitives, tokens, NFTs, and blockchain in the enterprise.

I believe *The Bytes Behind the Blocks* is a must-read for anyone starting to learn about blockchain or for those needing a refresher on the latest developments and future opportunities. But most especially, this book can provide tremendous value for those needing help with the most-asked question in business: Is blockchain right for you?

If you are a lover of blockchain, technology, or even just knowledge, you are in for an eye-opening journey!

INTRODUCTION

We live in interesting times. As I write this, the world has experienced multiple phases of a pandemic, Bitcoin has pulled back from its recent all-time high of $70,000 USD, TikTok is everywhere, and the pace of technology changes serving digital transformation has reached levels not seen for some time. Organizations are having to reinvent themselves or face extinction, globalization is pervasive, and consumers are moving toward online and digital-first experiences.

To match these shifts, enterprise technology is shifting to cloud platforms including public, private, hybrid, and multi-cloud solutions. Artificial intelligence (AI) and machine learning (ML) are priorities, and data has become one of the most valuable enterprise assets—if not the most valuable. The Internet of Things (IoT), 5G, automation in various forms, low-code development, and extended reality are picking up steam, with advancements in quantum computing and autonomous software agents just around the corner.

In the midst of it all is a technology known as blockchain. Often associated with cryptocurrencies like Bitcoin and ETH, blockchain has an identity crisis. Is it purely for cryptocurrency speculators? A way to sidestep government and regulatory institutions? A replacement for current financial institutions and processes? Or something else? If something else, then what, and why does it matter to the enterprise of today and tomorrow?

If you wade through the vast amounts of blockchain whitepapers, articles, books, blogs, and conferences, you find descriptions of how to get rich investing in cryptocurrencies, how blockchain is the new internet, and how it will take over the world. Much of it comes from sources with a vested interest in convincing you their approach is the best, which doesn't always map to an enterprise solution. That's not to say these ideas are unimportant as a foundation for solving problems such as inequality, identity, and the "unbanked." But they are not the focus of this book.

WHY READ THIS BOOK?

Instead, this book attempts to wade through the piles of material, distill them into something easily consumable, and describe blockchain with an enterprise-first mindset. Enterprises today are complex entities with many challenges, including managing legacy systems, leveraging data, moving to the cloud, innovating while "keeping the lights on," managing a global workforce, responding to shifting customer demands, adapting to new supply chains, and many more.

For these organizations, it is important to understand the why. *Why does blockchain make sense, why should it be considered, and why is it relevant outside of cryptocurrency?* Adding to the confusion is a lack of standardization and growing choices in blockchain architectures, technology components, frameworks, languages, and implementation models.

Blockchain isn't the answer to everything, but in some cases, it *could* be the answer, and the enterprise needs a solid, vendor-agnostic source of information to make this determination.

THIS BOOK IS THAT SOURCE.

It doesn't focus on cryptocurrency, specific framework features, or coding examples. Neither does it endorse a specific vendor or try to oversell the merits of blockchain. But if you need to understand blockchain's core concepts, relevance to the enterprise, or potential fit for data management, identity, privacy, tokenization, Web3, and more, it will be a useful guide. A "one-stop shop" for the chief technology officer (CTO) or architects in your organization.

Of course, blockchain involves more than technology. In addition to providing a practical guide on various technical concepts and use cases, I cover what you need to think about when selecting, implementing, and managing a blockchain solution. What are some common myths and misconceptions? How do you determine if a blockchain is the right choice? And what do you need to consider when selecting a blockchain solution? The answers are just as important as the technology itself.

Blockchain encompasses many acronyms, algorithms, buzzwords, concepts, and languages. A discussion of consensus alone would fill a book! The technology, regulations, and use cases are also changing rapidly, almost daily. While we can't possibly cover everything related to blockchain in this book, we can arm you with the knowledge to make your own choices. Thinking about blockchain requires a shift in mindset, and the path will be bumpy. This book will hopefully smooth out the ride.

Happy reading!

Chapter 1

WHY BLOCKCHAIN FOR THE ENTERPRISE?

This chapter is the beginning of your blockchain journey. As with many technologies, blockchain has humble beginnings, making an entrance before newsworthy phenomena such as Bitcoin, decentralized finance, non-fungible tokens, self-sovereign identity, Web3, and dApps came on the scene. Originally designed to address challenges such as the Byzantine Generals Problem,[2] blockchain, along with features such as consensus and distributed ledgers, looks at maintaining security, agreement, privacy, and trust across a distributed network. Blockchain addresses various issues in this context, and ensures such a network continues to function normally, even in the face of adversity.

---

[2] Leslie Lamport, Robert Shostak, and Marshall Pease, "The Byzantine Generals Problem," *ACM Transactions on Programming Language and Systems* 4, no. 3 (July 1982): 382-401, https://doi.org/10.1145/357172.357176.

You will find, however, many conflicting opinions about blockchain. From "It's nothing more than a solution looking for a problem" to "It will become as pervasive as the internet and completely change the way we live." While I don't pretend to have a crystal ball, I do have a practical view of blockchain and its potential applicability for the enterprise—and a desire to provide a strong foundation so you can determine if blockchain is something you want to pursue for your organization.

But before we delve into its many technologies and concepts, it's important to understand why you should at least be aware of these concepts in the first place. Why is blockchain relevant to the enterprise? What industry trends are driving this discussion? And where is blockchain headed? By the end of this chapter, you'll have the answer to these questions, after which we'll dig deeper into blockchain concepts, use cases, and future potential—the subjects addressed in the remainder of this book.

THE "WHY" FOR THE ENTERPRISE

Enterprises today are under tremendous and continuous pressure—to operate in the face of rapidly changing global conditions, respond to shifting customer behavior and priorities, keep pace with evolving technology, manage sensitive data, and conform to regulations that are sometimes unclear and conflicting. Behind these pressures are various industry trends that are creating much of the interest in blockchain and influencing how organizations approach digital transformation and deliver products and services.

We'll get to these trends, but first, we need a simple definition of blockchain. (Even this is fairly contentious, depending on the background of the people providing the detail. Some groups refer to the Bitcoin network as the only true blockchain, while others use the term as a buzzword to drive approval of IT projects.) For our purposes, we'll take the middle road, then spend the rest of this book describing the definition's twists and turns. Remember, we are focused on the enterprise use of blockchains, which is often described differently than in the cryptocurrency space, and so we'll use this definition:

Blockchain is a decentralized data management platform where, along with embedded business logic and trust, data can be securely and transparently shared across a distributed network of participants.

This, of course, is just one definition, and I'm sure it's already causing some debate in your mind! But we need to start somewhere, and I find it mostly, if not entirely, understandable by people familiar with enterprise IT concepts. We will drill down into the key words to provide a deeper understanding of the meaning and implications in later chapters. But for now, let's keep this definition handy while looking at five industry trends driving blockchain interest and its use in the enterprise.

Trend #1: Highly Connected Interactions

Businesses no longer operate in a vacuum, serve only local customers, and source from relatively local suppliers. Today's enterprises are global, highly connected, and able to serve customers at any location at any time. In this environment, they need to share data and processes related to product movement, invoice payments, order fulfillment, and a vast number of other needs that drive business-to-business (B2B) interactions.

Ideally, these interactions are highly automated to reduce time and effort, as well as seamlessly integrated into the various systems that support them. But unfortunately, as with many of today's solutions, these automation and integration goals are not met. Processes are manual and slow, data is shared in a cumbersome and sometimes unsecure fashion, and each organization has multiple versions of the truth spread across datastores. Bulk file transfers, electronic data interchange (EDI) platforms, direct API links, and even old-fashioned paper are used to share data. Process steps are often disjointed, inefficient, and/or duplicated.

This situation is not conducive to providing timely, contextual, trusted, and accurate information, and it negatively impacts the customer experience. Data becomes unreliable and out-of-sync, and regulatory compliance issues can arise as a result. Furthermore, as the world becomes more connected through technologies such as 5G[3] and IoT, the problem only gets worse. Clearly, a better way of "doing B2B" is needed.

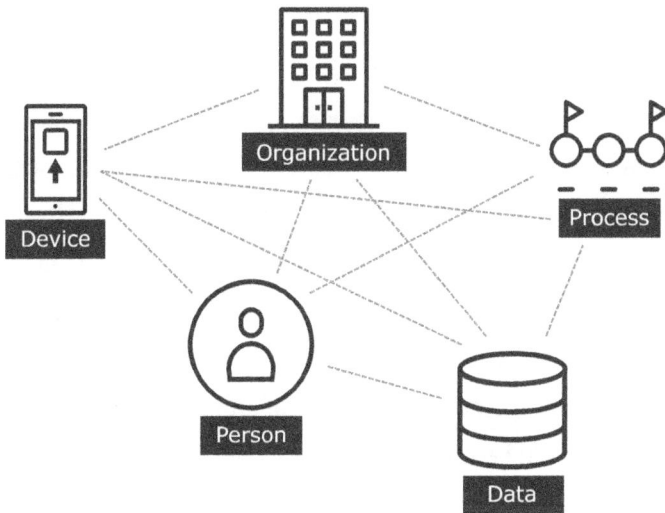

Today's world is highly connected and interactive.

Of course, it is not enough to do the same thing in only a slightly better way. To remain competitive and relevant, enterprises need to constantly review and adjust to change created by their customers, the market, and various other factors and conditions. An enterprise's review of changing conditions may result in adjustments to

---

[3] Wikipedia, s.v. "5G," last modified May 31, 2022, 13:13 (UTC), https://en.wikipedia.org/wiki/5G.

its current strategy or drastic pivots to new business models and enabling processes. It cannot take years to make these changes. Organizations need a solid technical and process foundation within their walls and among all participants that comprise their end-to-end value chain.

The need for trusted, secure, verifiable, and near real-time data sharing and process execution across multiple parties is one area that blockchain attempts to address. I use "attempts" because the solution is not simple, and other factors drive the use of blockchain in this context, which will be discussed in later chapters. However, the core characteristics of blockchain as defined above make it a technology option in situations involving multiple, distributed participants, shared data, automated processes, and a degree of trust and transparency. And as the number of interactions increases, the more blockchain becomes an option.

Trend #2: Decentralized Business Networks

Over time, business transactions involving multiple parties tend to evolve to include intermediate third parties that provide functions such as governance, regulation monitoring, payment services, broker services, and mediation. For example, many insurance companies use insurance brokers to interact with customers, real estate transactions are facilitated by a real estate agent, and many financial transactions are validated, recorded, or settled through a third party.

Perhaps you've heard that blockchain provides an opportunity to completely eliminate the middleman, the thought being that third parties introduce problems[4] for a business network: additional security risks, the need for implicit trust in their abilities and timeliness, increased transaction costs and processing time, and a lack of control in how a service outage is resolved. Without third parties, the thought continues, the process would be more streamlined, cost-efficient, transparent, and trusted. Bitcoin is the typical example provided to demonstrate how such a network could successfully operate.

However, a key item to remember is that the Bitcoin network is self-contained. External parties, or entities not participating in the protocol, are not creating new coins, and the ledger is the only valid source for identifying Bitcoin ownership. The rules of the network govern transaction validity, so there is no need for a third party to do it.

Enterprises, of course, do not operate in self-contained or closed-loop environments. Given various dependencies, such as government regulations, technology, financial systems, legal frameworks, and many other functions, it is not always possible to completely eliminate the middleman.

---

[4] Nick Szabo, "Trusted Third Parties are Security Holes," Satoshi Nakamoto Institute, 2005, https://nakamotoinstitute.org/trusted-third-parties/.

For example, with many types of business processes, you need to verify the identity of the individual initiating the process. This step is typically done using documents provided by a trusted third party, including passports, driver's licenses, and other credentials. Note there are approaches, commonly referred to as self-sovereign identity (SSI) or decentralized identity, that use a blockchain to capture and share this type of information. (Identity is covered in more detail later.) While these approaches can streamline the verification process and subsequently put the power of identity back into the hands of its owner, verifying traditional identity before a party is registered on a blockchain still requires some form of trusted third party.

Another example of not being able to eliminate the middleman is the supply chain. There are many examples of organizations looking at blockchain technology as a way to track the provenance of goods and materials, including food products, precious minerals, and cargo. Information about the tracked item is recorded on the blockchain as it moves through the supply chain, and all related parties subsequently receive a trusted, up-to-date view of the item's status through the blockchain network. In many cases, IoT devices and inputs from other external sources provide or augment the data needed for this end-to-end view. Sounds great, right? But even here, the need for a third party is not necessarily eliminated. Who validates the creation of the product to be tracked in the first place? Can the IoT devices be trusted? How is information about the item produced? The answer to all these questions is often "by a trusted third party." It's true that you may be able to build trust for a single entity through quorums or programmable agreements among multiple parties or devices, but these interactions only reduce the concern; they don't eliminate it.

Given these examples, is a blockchain relevant in building decentralized business networks without third parties? At least for the immediate future, trusted third parties are probably needed to provide or validate data, verify ownership, resolve disputes, or even validate the implementation of the blockchain network itself. However, this doesn't mean that blockchain technology provides no value in this context. Too many third parties, or too much centralization, tightens dependencies, increases costs, forms brittle networks, and negatively impacts time to market. Blockchain may not eliminate the middleman completely, but it can streamline interactions with third parties, such as collecting and distributing data, automating processes, governing behavior, programmatically representing transaction logic, or providing a common view of data across all participants. This streamlining can obviously have a positive impact on enterprise functions, minimize third-party dependencies, and lead to customer benefits.

A note before moving on: You are probably thinking that you can do all this with a shared or distributed database, so why even consider blockchain? Definitely a valid point, and true in many cases, as we will see in later chapters. More to come on this topic, as it is probably one of the most asked questions when considering blockchain in the enterprise!

Trend #3: The Need for "Abilities"

Building enterprise architectures and systems is hard. You don't have the luxury of rewriting or replacing applications every couple of years; innovation needs to roll out on whatever systems you have. In addition, technology is constantly evolving, business demands never stop, and you operate under cost, resource, and time constraints. Systems have to be deployed with appropriate levels of integrity, security, transparency, scalability, resiliency, and interoperability. Transactions must be streamlined, and regulatory and legal requirements for privacy, information sharing, personal data, and various others must be followed. Add vast amounts of data from many disparate sources, evolving cloud topologies, IoT proliferation, and the odd global disruption, and the enterprise can be a very complex environment indeed!

Blockchain is not the solution to all of these challenges, but depending on the framework, it can offer benefits for enterprise architectures and solutions. Distributed, fault-tolerant, tamper-resistant and append-only data storage, embedded business logic, agreed-upon transactions, elevated transparency, and various other features have the potential to provide immense value to an organization, both now and in the future. The principles and approaches associated with blockchain solutions can also encourage new thinking about business problems and lead to new business models and opportunities. All of these "abilities" can be valuable as your organization transitions to a digital-first mindset.

Trend #4: The Need to Innovate

Innovation is not easy, but it also cannot stop. Enterprises need to continuously innovate within their industry and across others. As such, it's important to be aware of technologies like blockchain, and take a practical view of its potential for your industry and use cases. I've seen many situations where an organization hasn't stayed abreast of emerging technology and simply becomes unable to keep up with competitors when delivering products and services. Remember, however, to avoid the hype and what I call "architecture by resume"! Blockchain doesn't solve every problem, and like any technology, it should be evaluated based on its merits, not on the surrounding noise.

Blockchain, of course, is not the only trend out there, but it has enough momentum, interest, and staying power to exist in one form or another as time passes. In my opinion, blockchain should be one of those technologies on your list to monitor and experiment with.

Trend #5: The Need for Community and Collaboration

By their very nature, blockchain solutions drive collaboration. If you are looking to deploy blockchain for a use case that does not involve more than one participant, you're very likely looking at the wrong solution.

A large part of blockchain's value comes from the presence of multiple participants, but in many cases, the creation of associated consortiums or private/permissioned blockchain networks can be more complicated than the technology itself. This is one reason why certain blockchain projects appear to go quiet for a time. The legal aspects and governance models among those involved can be challenging to define, a topic I expand on later.

You will typically encounter two types of blockchain communities. One is interested in the technology itself: Hyperledger, the Enterprise Ethereum Alliance (EEA), the Trusted IoT Alliance, and others drive blockchain advancements to address its limitations and broaden its applicability in various use cases. The other type is interested in blockchain for use in particular business spaces: B3i (insurance), MOBI (mobility), Food Trust (supply chain), Global Blockchain Business Council (advocacy/education/standards), Global Shipping Business Network (shipping), Hashed Health (healthcare), and we.trade (finance) are examples.

It is also useful to note that several governments and agencies have formed blockchain organizations. The Australian government has established a national roadmap for blockchain and associated standards, regulations, skills, capabilities, investment, and collaboration. The World Health Organization (WHO) has partnered with other organizations to address problems related to information and data sharing. And the World Economic Forum (WEF) has established a platform for blockchain, digital assets, and data policy. Many other examples exist as governments look at associated concerns such as regulation, privacy, digital currencies, tokenization, and asset ownership.

Regardless of the type of community, there is the realization that, for blockchain to succeed, both the technology and the understanding of its potential need to evolve. Progress is best advanced through collaboration and communities providing scale, strength in numbers, and potential for standardization.

FINAL THOUGHTS

Blockchain technology and opinions about it change rapidly, especially on its use in enterprises. It has its fair share of hype, and its applicability in the organization is often blurred by discussions on cryptocurrencies and various types of "coins." While these discussions are relevant, enterprises also need to look widely at the opportunity for its use in other areas of the business.

Problems related to information sharing, automation, collaboration, transparency, and real-time visibility in decentralized business networks are all possible opportunities for blockchain to provide value. Many types of business transactions would benefit from a better way of "doing B2B," one that provides improvements in efficiency, cost, and time.

Blockchain is not for everyone or every problem. But it is my hope that this chapter provided sufficient detail as to why it should not be ignored and that you will continue this journey as I explore potential ways to apply the technology.

Chapter 2

USE CASE MATCHES MADE IN HEAVEN

Blockchain has struggled to find its killer value proposition. Just a few short years ago, it was receiving a large amount of hype, organizations were suffering from FOMO,[5] and it was being positioned as the solution for everything! If "blockchain" was included in a project proposal or mentioned in an investor meeting, the presenter was likely to receive extra attention, project approval, and additional funding.

However, as knowledge and experience with the technology increased, enterprises have realized blockchain is not the answer to every problem. Organizations like Microsoft and IBM (at the time of this writing) have even scaled back their blockchain offerings; the promise of huge enterprise-derived revenues has not been realized.

---

[5] Fear of missing out

Blockchain finance and tokenization are very active, but noise around enterprise use cases has certainly subsided. Certain groups and individuals point to the lack of success stories as proof that blockchain is simply not needed in the enterprise, and alternative approaches such as cloud databases or APIs are sufficient. Does this mean blockchain is dead to the enterprise?

As discussed in Chapter 1, industry trends are pointing to the need for solutions that are highly connected, decentralized, capable, collaborative, and innovative. While it is certainly true that blockchain cannot solve all enterprise problems, I believe it does have its place in the industry, so this chapter discusses use cases where it has either been implemented successfully or proposed as a solution to a common problem. I will reserve judgment on its fit for these use cases until Chapter 10, when I cover enterprise architectures and associated selection criteria. For now, on to the examples.

Blockchain is past the initial hype stage, which is a positive step because focus can now shift to real-world problems and evolving the technology as experience and creativity grow. By the end of this chapter, with use cases ranging from making a process "better" to more forward-thinking applications, you will start to see where blockchain might fit.

MULTI-PARTY PROCESS AUTOMATION

Enterprise use cases involving multiple parties are one of the most obvious choices for blockchain. A need to share data and execute business logic in a way that's secure, trusted, and agreed upon among distributed participants is key to success in these scenarios. As a result, supply chain, transportation, insurance, healthcare, and other areas have deployed blockchain typically in permissioned form and under the governance of a consortium. These solutions tend to fall under the "better way of doing B2B" category, although in some cases the benefits are realized from the acts of automating manual processes and digitalizing paper, not necessarily because of the use of blockchain. Although non-technical considerations, such as the consortium structure and governing rules, can be just as challenging as the technology, under the right circumstances, blockchain provides value, which is why use cases involving multi-party business processes are popular enterprise use case examples.

Healthcare and Insurance

Healthcare and insurance blockchain use cases tend to focus on two main issues: (1) the desire to create a digital identifier that securely represents and verifies an individual while maintaining appropriate privacy levels, and (2) the need to reduce the time, cost, and effort spent on business processes involving multiple parties. I look at the problem of identity in Chapter 8, but in short, blockchain is one possible solution to the problems associated with securely sharing personal or organizational credentials and identities. This includes blockchain's use in electronic health records, medical records, claims processing, healthcare provider registries, and more.

The need to streamline and automate healthcare and insurance processes also receives a lot of attention given aging populations in many countries, rising costs, process time delays, and a lack of synchronized data among all participants. Claims processing, claim verification, automated claim payouts, patient or client journey tracking, transaction auditing, and prescription drug provenance are all examples of multi-party business processes that can benefit from blockchain capabilities.

For example, Change Healthcare, a healthcare technology company in the United States, is investigating the use of blockchain to automate claims processing.[6] In Singapore, insurance provider MetLife has trialed a blockchain-based insurance product that allows payouts to be expedited and automated.[7] Groups such as B3i (https://b3i .tech/home.html) and Hashed Health (https://hashedhealth.com/) are looking at providing blockchain solutions and distributed ledgers for these industries.

---

[6] Change Healthcare, homepage, accessed May 10, 2022, https://www.changehealthcare.com/about/innovation/blockchain.

[7] Business Wire, "MetLife's New Blockchain Health Insurance Product Eliminates Claims," August 20, 2018, https://www.businesswire.com/news/home/20180820005644/en/.

The COVID-19 pandemic also highlighted the need for improved information sharing, health agency coordination, outbreak tracking, and alerting. This led to the creation of MiPasa (https://app.mipasa .com/), a platform built on Hyperledger Fabric to facilitate sharing of pandemic information between need-to-know organizations. Other, more general blockchain solutions addressing the problem of multi-party information sharing and analytics are further described in Chapter 9.

Of course, the use of blockchain in healthcare and insurance is not without challenges, including lingering security concerns, regulatory uncertainty, privacy considerations, performance limitations, legal guidelines, and the need for appropriate data management strategies. The status quo in these industries cannot continue, however, because budgets and time are not unlimited, providing an opportunity for disruption via blockchain.

Supply Chain and Product Provenance

Supply chain and product provenance use cases are currently some of the most common enterprise applications of blockchain. Traditional supply chain processes are often slow and disjointed, common infrastructure is non-existent, multiple parties are required to collaborate, and proper completion of key process steps is often difficult to verify. Data is inconsistent, and obtaining a single, timely view of information across all parties is challenging. There is also a growing consumer interest in the origin of the products they are consuming, which requires an elevated level of trust and visibility between product providers and purchasers.

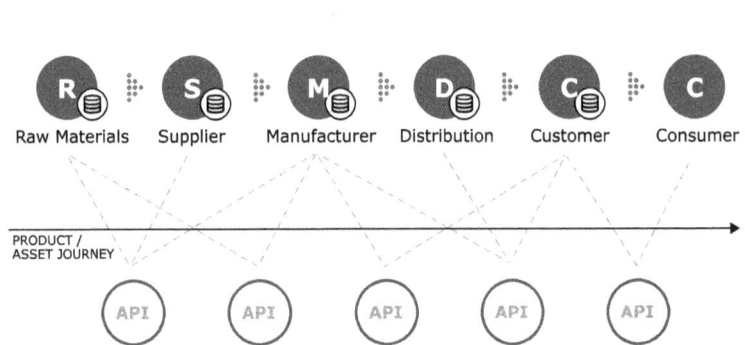

Current supply chain methods are point-to-point, out-of-sync, and manual.

To address these challenges, many organizations have turned to blockchain, offering several real-world use cases. IBM has built a blockchain-based solution for managing the complete food supply chain, incorporating participants such as producers, suppliers, manufacturers, and retailers. This permissioned network, referred to as IBM Food Trust (https://www.ibm.com/blockchain/solutions /food-trust), is based on Hyperledger Fabric and lists well-known organizations such as Walmart and Dole as users. A modified form of this solution, IBM's Transparent Supply (https://www.ibm.com /blockchain/solutions/transparent-supply), focuses on broader supply chain use cases.

Various other platforms, such as TradeLens (https://www.trade lens.com/) and GrainChain (https://www.grainchain.io/), with consortiums such as the Global Shipping Business Network (https://www.gsbn.trade/), also use blockchain to streamline the supply chain.

As with healthcare and insurance, there are still technical challenges with blockchain in the supply chain. Complex compliance needs, governance rules, and the breadth of rapidly evolving technology choices add to these challenges. Furthermore, we know that data on a blockchain is only as good as its source, which makes trusted processes critical for validating and verifying any data destined for the blockchain network. Finally, bringing together diverse organizations and reaching an agreement on the functioning of such a network can be time-consuming, often leading to the early departure of founding members or the development of alternative solutions.

However, as I will describe in the following chapters, blockchain offers the potential to address many of these issues. From its ability to replicate data with consensus across multiple parties, incorporate business logic in the form of smart contracts, minimize the need to directly trust each participant, and maintain a tamper-resistant history of transactions, blockchain provides capabilities beyond what may be found with typical distributed databases or other traditional solutions.

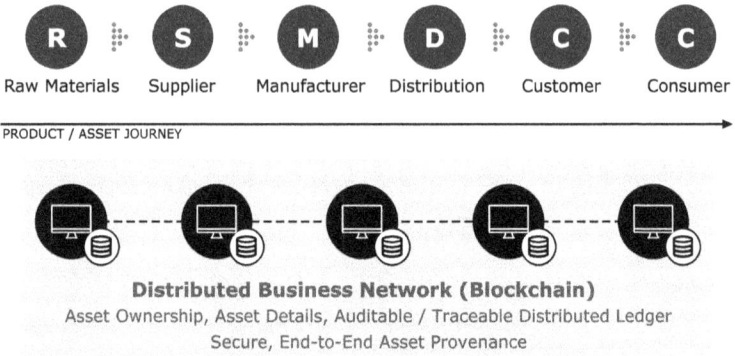

R	S	M	D	C	C
Raw Materials	Supplier	Manufacturer	Distribution	Customer	Consumer

PRODUCT / ASSET JOURNEY

Distributed Business Network (Blockchain)
Asset Ownership, Asset Details, Auditable / Traceable Distributed Ledger
Secure, End-to-End Asset Provenance

A connected supply chain network offers increased trust,
better tracking, and end-to-end visibility.

Consumer and Commercial Contracts

As I will discuss in Chapter 6, the degree to which legal or contract language can be captured in code varies,[8] with most solutions currently augmenting code with traditional text-based contracts. However, the opportunity to automate contract terms and associated actions or penalties is immense, with corresponding benefits such as reduced costs, improved response times, increased accuracy, and streamlined customer experiences.

Blockchain frameworks, especially those with smart contract capabilities, have the potential to solve various problems in this category.

---

[8] Nick Szabo, "Wet Code and Dry," *Unenumerated: An Unending Variety of Topics* (blog), August 24, 2008, https://unenumerated.blogspot.com/2006/11/wet-code-and-dry.html.

For example, blockchain could be used to:

- Streamline the processes for purchasing or leasing a vehicle. This could include verifying the purchaser's eligibility, acquiring insurance, tracking service history, or automating the purchase of related services such as a warranty plan. This use of blockchain was proposed by Visa and DocuSign in 2015,[9] and although it did not proceed due to challenges including public ledger storage costs and performance, the opportunity to automate customer transactions, especially complex transactions involving many parties and processes, still shows promise.

- Automate payouts of various types, including insurance payouts, flight delay compensation, medical claims, or penalties for nonperformance.

- Manage contracts related to the use of Distributed Energy Resources (DERs) to optimize the storage and redistribution of energy from sources such as wind and solar. Insolar attempted this use case in 2019/2020 but failed due to a lack of funding, too broad of a scope, and

---

[9] Stan Higgins, "Visa Debuts Bitcoin Proof-of-Concept for Car Leasing," *CoinDesk*, October 27, 2015, https://www.coindesk.com/visa-docusign-car-lease-proof-of-concept-bitcoin.

challenges in building an associated ecosystem.[10] However, the need to streamline and automate contracts associated with smart cities, smart buildings, and smart grids will only increase, opening many opportunities.

- Facilitate the execution of customs declarations, cross-border settlement transactions, or other types of transactions involving parties in different countries. With blockchain, there's the opportunity to minimize the number of intermediaries required in these scenarios, reduce fraud, and improve transaction completion times. One current example of this use case is RippleNet (https://ripple.com /ripplenet/), which aims to streamline payment services and simplify the ability of financial services organizations to move money globally.

Almost any complex, multi-party consumer or commercial contract represents an opportunity for blockchain. Further work is expected in this area, with organizations such as the Accord project (https:// accordproject.org/) and others specifically looking at the problem of building and executing smart legal contracts.

---

[10] Rachel Wolfson, "Enterprise Blockchain of Today: While Some Fail, Others Show Potential Value," *Cointelegraph*, February 18, 2021, https://cointelegraph.com/news /enterprise-blockchain-of-today-while-some-fail-others-show-potential-value.

OWNERSHIP

The problem of ownership, or determining who has rights to a particular asset, is an extremely complex topic. Ownership and property rights, copyright laws, physical versus digital assets, proof and verification of original ownership, shared or partial ownership, and the ability to transfer ownership are all important concepts to understand when attempting to represent ownership on blockchain. In most cases, the solution not only involves technology, but also various legal and regulatory considerations that differ between countries. Regardless, it is likely that a large amount of ownership rights, especially those that are public, will eventually be registered in some form of a blockchain.

I am not a lawyer, so unfortunately, I cannot help with the legal nuances of ownership. But the challenges present an opportunity for blockchain, although certain uses may have more obvious value than others: CryptoKicks?[11] For physical assets, it is feasible that blockchain could act as a verified, trusted, and agreed-upon source of ownership information. A complete ownership history could be maintained on a ledger backed by trusted entities who would provide verification of original ownership and perform functions such as dispute resolution. Transfers of ownership could then be facilitated through the use of smart contracts.

---

[11] NIKE, Inc., System and Method for Providing Cryptographically Secured Digital Assets, US Patent 10,505,726, filed May 28, 2019, and issued December 10, 2019, https://pdfpiw.uspto.gov/.piw?docid=10505726&PageNum=1&&IDKey=DEF6196CEC57.

Digital assets, such as music, art, and other content may also be represented on a blockchain, although the laws regulating these types of assets and associated ownership tend to lag behind what is occurring in the market. Thus, the definition of ownership in this context may not be clear or consistent, especially across countries. Ease of transferability, direct access by content creators to consumers, and programmable royalties are all areas in which blockchain could be applied to digital assets. In fact, these features are driving the current activity in the NFT (non-fungible token) market, a topic I cover in Chapter 11 when I look at tokenization.

BLOCKCHAIN WITH IOT

The world of IoT is growing rapidly, with technologies such as cloud, edge compute, and 5G sparking renewed interest in the deployment of devices for enhanced data collection, equipment control, predictive maintenance, and more. This proliferation of devices, however, leads to several challenges. How do you verify the identity of an IoT device? What measures can be put in place to ensure a device is not being spoofed? How can you achieve greater autonomy and collaboration between devices without requiring human involvement? Are there opportunities for new business models in this highly connected world of devices and networks?

There are technical solutions to these challenges, but many are based on point-to-point infrastructure, depend on connectivity to a centralized environment, or are deployed on expensive private networks and hardware. As device numbers (things) grow, these solutions will not be sufficient. First, it is not feasible to send all IoT data back to a remote cloud environment because the volume of data is substantial and not all of it is needed or wanted. Second, the amount of time it takes to send this data, perform necessary processing, and deliver a response is simply too long in many cases; the identified opportunity (cross-sell) or threat (equipment failure) is likely missed or has taken its toll. Third, coordinating large numbers of devices via centralized logic is challenging to achieve at the scale, cost, and latency values required.

There is a move towards pushing compute to the edge, including the deployment of analytical models closer to the data source. This scheme potentially minimizes the amount of data delivered to downstream systems and reduces the time needed for automated processing and decision-making. However, there is still a need to properly identify, verify, and secure the devices, as well as facilitate the creation of automated device networks where devices exchange capabilities to perform a task or achieve a result without human intervention.

The need for an integrated, distributed, and automated IoT network with trusted devices and no single attack vector or point of failure represents key opportunities for blockchain. The most obvious opportunity is to use a blockchain's distributed, tamper-resistant, and agreed-upon ledger as a store or hash of critical IoT data snapshots. This data can be valuable for many reasons, including input for the supply chain use cases previously mentioned, or for regulatory purposes. Next, smart contracts may be used to automatically execute logic in response to verified IoT data feeds. These contracts could perform a variety of tasks, including executing automated payments when certain contractual conditions are met, triggering alerts in response to a violation of service level agreements, or providing an end-to-end audit log of critical information.

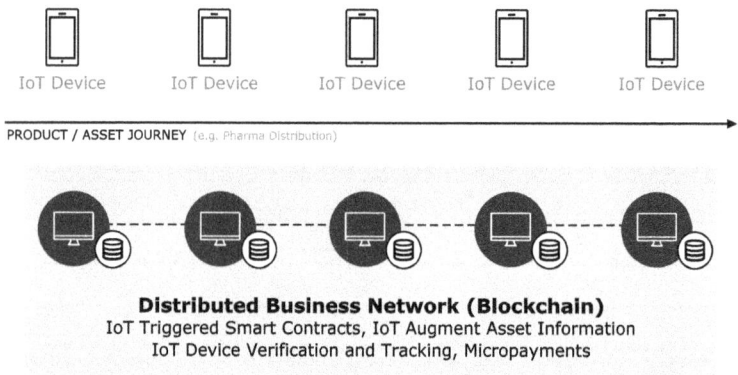

Distributed Business Network (Blockchain)
IoT Triggered Smart Contracts, IoT Augment Asset Information
IoT Device Verification and Tracking, Micropayments

IoT blockchain deployment enabling collaborative device networks

Other blockchain IoT opportunities involve device identity, verification, and security. Today, IoT devices—especially those deployed outside of an industrial context—often have security vulnerabilities. Various examples of device attacks[12] are available on the internet,

---

[12] Wikipedia, s.v. "DDoS attack on Dyn," last modified May 9, 2022, 05:49 (UTC), https://en.wikipedia.org/wiki/DDoS_attack_on_Dyn.

with many more likely occurring behind closed doors. A lack of standardization, mixed device environments, remote installations, and limited compute capabilities all make identifying, verifying, and securing devices challenging. I cover using blockchain to enhance identity in Chapter 8, as the technology applies not only to people and organizations, but also to devices.

And finally, blockchain could be used to facilitate forms of micro-payments, where devices "pay" each other for functions or data. Vehicle-to-vehicle or vehicle-to-infrastructure networks are examples that could benefit from this capability, where vehicles would "pay" while driving on inductive charging roads, sell stored electricity back to a power grid, or participate in swarm intelligence networks. These interactions provide the opportunity to create new business models, and further blend the digital and physical worlds for a more seamless and automated experience.

One interesting challenge with blockchain and IoT use cases is the need to use a consensus algorithm optimized for the needs of such a network. Common consensus approaches such as Proof of Work or Proof of Stake are not effective in an IoT context because they aren't designed to handle the number of devices likely to be attached to the network, do not support the low latency requirements needed for real-time IoT decision-making, lack immediate finality, and involve relatively high transaction costs. Instead, a new consensus algorithm, along with an application-specific blockchain platform, is needed at each layer of the IoT architecture, including the edge, gateway, and enterprise IoT layers. IOTA's Tangle protocol (https://www.iota.org/), currently under development, is an example of such an approach and will be covered briefly in Chapter 5. Tangle introduces a secure, peer-to-peer decentralized network based on a directed acyclic graph distributed ledger technology (DLT). It promises low resource requirements, zero-fee transactions, and relatively short transaction confirmation times, which would all benefit a distributed IoT network. Given the newness of this technology, limitations do exist, but this and other emerging frameworks are worth watching.

BLOCKCHAIN AND DIGITAL TWINS

Most people are familiar with the concept of digital twins in the context of the Internet of Things (IoT) or the Industrial Internet of Things (IIoT). Creating a software-based twin or shadow of a device or machine, and then manipulating and testing this model is substantially cheaper, faster, and safer than modifying the physical component itself. The impact of changes can be quickly determined, various combinations of input values and settings can be tested without requiring complex setup or access, and outputs can be optimized according to established goals before any change is made to the physical component.

The concept of a digital twin may also be applied to other real-world entities, including people, organizations, or business processes. For example, a digital twin can be created that represents a payment process, a maintenance procedure, a passenger, a customer, or even more complex systems such as supply chains, power grids with distributed energy resources (DERs), or smart cities. In all cases, the core benefits remain the same: enable a safer, cheaper, and faster way to manipulate and optimize the inputs and outputs to and from the digital twin before implementing these changes to the real-world entities.

Successfully implementing a digital twin, however, requires several capabilities. From process mining and integration services to analytics and event processing, building digital twins for the purposes of running simulations or supporting live, real-time execution can be a complex undertaking. While a discussion of each of these components is beyond the scope of this book, many digital twin implementations, especially those that run live and span multiple organizations, can benefit from blockchain. Tamper-resistant, replicated, and distributed data storage, automated logic via smart contracts, enhanced transparency and traceability, and minimal required trusted third parties all enhance a digital twin offering. In most cases, blockchain is combined with other capabilities as part of a larger architectural framework, as shown in the following diagram. Tracking products through a supply chain, automatically generating and capturing payments as contractual obligations are met, and recording equipment maintenance activities are examples of use cases that can benefit from a blockchain-backed digital twin.

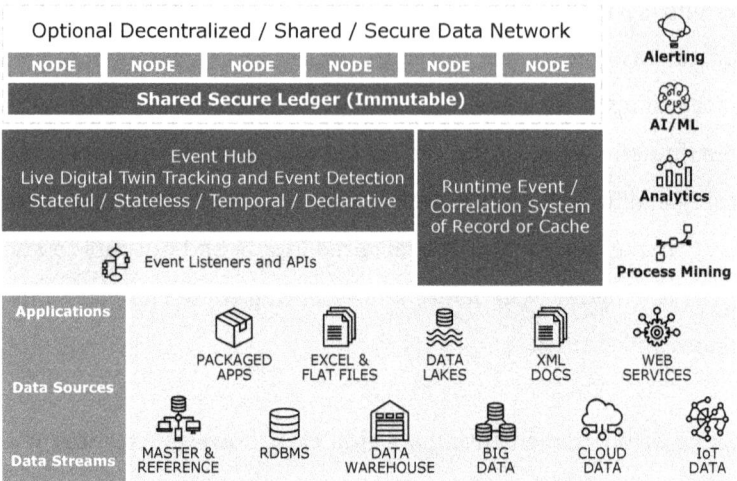

Optional Decentralized / Shared / Secure Data Network						Alerting
NODE	NODE	NODE	NODE	NODE	NODE	
Shared Secure Ledger (Immutable)						AI/ML
Event Hub Live Digital Twin Tracking and Event Detection Stateful / Stateless / Temporal / Declarative				Runtime Event / Correlation System of Record or Cache		Analytics
Event Listeners and APIs						Process Mining
Applications	PACKAGED APPS	EXCEL & FLAT FILES	DATA LAKES	XML DOCS	WEB SERVICES	
Data Sources						
Data Streams	MASTER & REFERENCE	RDBMS	DATA WAREHOUSE	BIG DATA	CLOUD DATA	IoT DATA

Digital twin component architecture, including blockchain

As digital twins become more complex and network complexities increase, it is possible that blockchain will (in some form) become a more prevalent component of a digital twin runtime architecture.

FINANCE

Finance-related use cases are the other most obvious application for blockchain. Initial coin offerings (ICOs), the acceptance of crypto for consumer purchases, cryptocurrency exchanges, non-fungible tokens (NFTs), central bank digital currencies (CBDCs), decentralized finance (DeFi), various token types, and others are just a few related examples. I discuss some of these items in Chapter 11, but as mentioned, the intent of this book is to not get lost in the cryptocurrency discussion. Instead, in this chapter, I will highlight other possibilities for blockchain in finance, and leave the in-depth discussion of digital currencies for another time.

As with the other use cases mentioned in this chapter, the desire to eliminate manual, fragmented, time-consuming, and siloed business processes represents an opportunity for blockchain in finance. For example, the need to share allowlists, denylists, or other key reference data elements among financial organizations to reduce fraud or money laundering is one possibility for blockchain. Opportunities to improve processes related to functions such as cross-border payments and settlement, and to securely record transactions with consensus, offer assistance with custody and asset tracking. Payments, trade finance, and capital markets also suggest opportunities for blockchain capabilities.

Various organizations, including banks, fintechs, central banks, insurance companies, and others are undertaking blockchain research projects. The Depository Trust & Clearing Corporation (DTCC, https://www.dtcc.com/), a provider of various financial capabilities—from trade processing and clearing services to settlement, asset, wealth, and data services—is reviewing the use of blockchain for enhancing post-trade processes and streamlining support for private market securities.[13] The online business we.trade (https://we-trade.com) is a consortium of 16 banks across

---

[13] Depository Trust & Clearing Corporation, "DTCC Unveils Proposals to Explore Further Digitalization in the Public & Private Markets," May 18, 2020, https://www.dtcc.com/news/2020/may/18/dtcc-unveils-proposals-to-explore-further-digitalization.

15 countries founded to improve trade finance processes, while Mastercard and Visa are working to bring cryptocurrencies to payments. In some cases, this work is driven by market pressures as consumers shift to competitive products to execute transactions. In other cases, it is driven by the desire to improve current financial systems and bring new products to the market. Regardless, it is obvious that blockchain, along with global interest in digital currencies, is driving a large amount of research and innovation in finance.

The pairing of finance and blockchain could easily be a book itself, and I have only scratched the surface of the work being done. Other examples include corporations investing directly in cryptocurrencies, with companies such as MicroStrategy[14] and Block (previously Square)[15] holding Bitcoin on their balance sheet, and PayPal offering consumers the ability to use cryptocurrency for payment. There are also rumors (at the time of this writing) of organizations such as Amazon or Alphabet investigating the creation of their own digital currency. These advancements will place pressure on traditional institutions and governments, further accelerating the pace of innovation.

---

[14] "Bitcoin for Corporations," MicroStrategy website, https://www.microstrategy.com/en/bitcoin/bitcoin-for-corporations.

[15] Zack Guzman, "Square Buys $170 Million More in Bitcoin to Boost Crypto Holdings," Yahoo Finance, February 23, 2021, https://ca.finance.yahoo.com/news/square-buys-170-million-more-in-bitcoin-to-boost-crypto-holdings-222926163.html.

FINAL THOUGHTS

While not all use cases are made in heaven, opportunities do exist in the enterprise to use blockchain as part of a solution. I didn't even mention government, manufacturing, mining, intellectual property rights management, and loyalty programs, as some of the world's largest organizations currently participate in blockchain research.[16] It is also interesting to consider other scenarios, such as whether there is a need for data to outlive an organization. If a company goes out of business, what happens to its data? Blockchain may offer an opportunity to keep this data "alive" longer, through decentralization and distribution.

Challenges do exist, including technology maturity, performance, ease of use, cost and complexity of running a permissioned network and of executing transactions against a public network, and of selecting the right use case. As with any technology, a strong value proposition is required—preferably one not easily achievable without blockchain.

Will blockchain mature fast enough to keep pace with today's digital transformation initiatives? Will governance and regulatory issues outweigh the value of the technology? Or will blockchain evolve, encourage organizations to address these problems head-on,

---

[16] "Blockchain 50 2021," *Forbes*, February 2, 2021,
https://www.forbes.com/sites/michaeldelcastillo/2021/02/02/blockchain-50.

and deliver the next generation of highly connected digital applications? Given the amount of related research and work in the market today, along with current digital trends, I wouldn't bet against the technology yet!

Chapter 3

WHAT EXACTLY IS A BLOCKCHAIN?

Like many emerging technologies, blockchain brings with it a seemingly endless array of acronyms, terms, and concepts. Some of these are specific to blockchain, while others have been used in IT for some time and are now being applied in a blockchain context.

This chapter shifts from the "why" to the "what" and covers topics commonly associated with blockchains. I stay away from vendor-specific terms, but include concepts such as distributed ledgers, smart contracts, consensus, hashing, and oracles. Starting with the basics is key to understanding how a blockchain operates and, besides, if I tried to cover every single topic or term, this chapter would be extremely long! Follow along, and don't worry if something doesn't seem to fit at this point. We will drill down on other terms later in the book. "Mimblewimble" anyone?

STARTING WITH BLOCKCHAIN

To start, let's revisit our definition of blockchain from Chapter 1:

> **Blockchain** is a **decentralized data management platform** where, along with **embedded business logic** and **trust**, data may be **securely and transparently shared** across a **distributed network** of **participants**.

The first and most obvious term from this definition is "blockchain." It can be described broadly, as above, and also through a number of technical components.

To start, let's look at blockchain as one form of distributed ledger technology, otherwise referred to as a DLT. A blockchain DLT consists of an append-only data structure,[17] where data is shared across a network of blockchain participants or nodes through a peer-to-peer replication mechanism. The append-only aspect is an important quality helping to ensure that data cannot be deleted or updated. This feature has various benefits as I will show, but for enterprises dealing with issues such as data privacy, General Data Protection Regulation (GDPR), and the right of an individual to be "forgotten," it should be remembered when determining what data to store on-chain (in the blockchain ledger) or off-chain (outside the

---

[17] BitcoinWiki, s.v. "Merkle tree," last modified January 23, 2022, 22:40 (UTC), https://en.bitcoinwiki.org/wiki/Merkle_tree.

blockchain ledger). I further cover this topic in Chapter 5 when we look at DLT technology and other storage approaches such as ledger databases, and also through related discussions of zero-knowledge proofs later in the book.

Going deeper, this blockchain DLT data structure consists of a series of data "blocks" cryptographically linked via hashes to form a "chain."

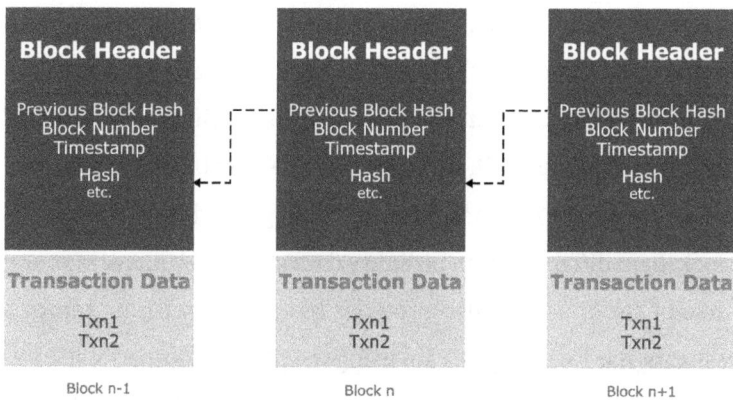

Block Header	**Block Header**	**Block Header**
Previous Block Hash Block Number Timestamp Hash etc.	Previous Block Hash Block Number Timestamp Hash etc.	Previous Block Hash Block Number Timestamp Hash etc.
Transaction Data Txn1 Txn2	**Transaction Data** Txn1 Txn2	**Transaction Data** Txn1 Txn2
Block n-1	Block n	Block n+1

Blockchain DLT data structure

Within each data block are a number of data elements, including a header with metadata, a set of transactions, and the previous block's hash. The current block hash is also included, which is derived from the block's data combined with the hash from the previous block.

To create these hashes, common IT industry techniques are used to quickly create a fingerprint or unique checksum for a set of data. From a hash, the original input data cannot be recreated; it is very difficult to create the same hash for two different inputs, and the identical input will always lead to the identical hash. Various algorithms are used for hashing, with SHA-256 a common approach in blockchain frameworks.

These hashes are critical because they can be used to quickly determine if any data in a block has changed, or if anyone has attempted to tamper with the chain. Because the hash of the current block contains the hash from the previous block, an attempt to, for example, insert a bad block in the middle of the chain will be obvious; the chain of hashes will be broken by the new block. This feature is a key element of blockchain technology, and it's what makes blockchain different from ordinary data structures like arrays and linked lists. The hash also provides blockchain with its tamper-resistant nature. And yes, I am using the phrase "tamper-resistant" and not "immutable" at this point, which is often how blockchain is described in the community. Immutability involves more than the use of cryptographic hashing and this data structure, a topic I explore further in Chapter 4.

With this background, we can now look at the other technical aspects associated with blockchain and our definition.

DECENTRALIZATION FOR THE ENTERPRISE

The second key term in our definition is "decentralization." What does it mean to be decentralized, and how does this apply to the enterprise?

To answer, we need to consider two elements of the technology: the architecture of the deployment, and the governance or operational structure of the network. Architecturally, a blockchain is decentralized, deployed across multiple machines or nodes rather than on a centralized server. No single node controls the network, there is no single point of failure, and data is shared across participants via peer-to-peer communication mechanisms. These qualities are also often referred to as a distributed architecture, which is common in large enterprises and used to address problems involving large amounts of data or business transactions.

The second aspect—governance or operational structure of the network—is more nuanced. In an enterprise context, a blockchain is typically not fully decentralized in its operations, but actually governed by a centralized group of individuals or companies. This group, referred to as a consortium, sets the rules as to who can join or leave the network, handles disputes, defines information exchanges, and formalizes cross-party business logic. This control results in a blockchain deployment that may be decentralized technically, but centralized in operation. Enterprises also have to collaborate with other centralized parties, including various regulatory, financial, or legal organizations, and this structure impacts the level of decentralization achievable by enterprise blockchains.

To elaborate on the concept of decentralization, we can look at who can read, write, or participate in the network. If the identity of the participants is not known, and if anyone can join the network, then the network is an open, public, or permissionless blockchain. Bitcoin is an example: anyone can participate, participants are largely pseudonymous, and there is no pre-existing trust between users.

Conversely, if participant identity is known before joining the network, access is controlled, and an established level of trust is pre-existing, the network is a closed, private, or permissioned blockchain. This is currently the most common form of blockchain in the enterprise, and it is the focus of this book. However, as blockchain technology advances, and additional use cases are tested, the lines between public and private blockchains are blurring.

For example, a permissioned network may allow anyone to join as long as they register with a verified set of credentials. This practice makes the network permissioned, but not private. Furthermore, some technology stacks incorporate capabilities from various types of blockchains into a single platform; for example, use cases such as decentralized finance (DeFi) involve representing financial instruments on a public blockchain. Also, many enterprise software companies are integrating traditional applications with public blockchains as a way to extend their capabilities into a permissionless network. We can definitely expect this blending of approaches to continue in the future.

DATA MANAGEMENT WITH BLOCKCHAIN

Data management and blockchain is an interesting combination. We earlier introduced blockchain as a form of DLT, and more detail will be provided in Chapter 5. For now, recognize that while blockchain may be a type of distributed ledger, not every distributed ledger is a blockchain. Remember the discussions on hashing, the creation of a chain of blocks, and decentralization? These elements are hints as to the differences between a DLT and a blockchain.

It is also important to recognize that the way data is stored and managed tends to differ between permissionless and permissioned networks. First, with enterprise blockchains, or more specifically frameworks targeted at permissioned networks, the technology that supports these implementations does not necessarily require all data to be duplicated on all nodes. In some cases, only certain participants need to see each other's data, so many blockchain frameworks allow private or participant-specific data sharing.

Second, enterprises need to determine which and how much data to store, its visibility, and the regulations pertaining to it. For example, it might not make sense to store data containing personal information in an append-only shared data structure. Large datasets, or data with complex relationships, may also not be a fit, given current limitations of blockchain frameworks and the associated charac-teristics of data sharing, peer-to-peer replication, consensus, and other related processing. For the enterprise, the question of what to store on-chain versus off-chain is a common one that requires careful consideration.

SHARING DATA SECURELY
AND TRANSPARENTLY

A large portion of blockchain's proposed value comes from its ability to openly and transparently share data and allow protocol partic-ipants to verify transactions and review the network's embedded business logic. With most open public blockchains, transparency is seen as a benefit; anyone can verify the behavior of the network and see if anything strange is occurring.

For enterprise use cases, complete transparency is not always desired. It may be advantageous to only share data between certain parties, or encrypt certain data elements so they are only acces-sible by participants with the right credentials or keys. The need for enterprise blockchains to have some form of privacy is why certain blockchain frameworks support the creation of private data not shared with everyone. While this is critical for the enter-prise, it does go against the historical premise of blockchain and leads to many debates on whether it's a true blockchain. For now, I'm just recognizing this need, and its importance in enterprise deployments.

Key Pairs and Digital Signatures

Previously, we discussed how hashing is used to establish the chain behind blockchain, and how the chain exposes attempts to tamper with or change verified data. However, we also want to prove and validate the provider of this data, and to possibly encrypt associated data elements. This is the role of public key cryptography, otherwise known as asymmetric cryptography, and the use of private keys, public keys, and digital signatures.

While a full description of public key cryptography (PKC) schemes, including RSA and elliptic curve cryptography (ECC), is beyond the scope of this book, it is important to understand the use of PKC in the context of blockchain. Public key cryptography involves the use of two mathematically related keys, referred to as public and private keys. Public keys are derived from private keys using a one-way operation; it is computationally difficult to reverse the process and compute the private key from the public key. This is important because the private key is meant to be kept secret and represents a particular user or participant in the network.

Once the public key is created, it can be distributed publicly across the network and used to encrypt data meant only for the corresponding private key holder, or to verify that a digitally signed message was originally created by the holder of the private key. As long as the private key is not stolen or lost, a recipient of a transaction can verify the authenticity of the sender, or be assured of the privacy of any data signed and sent to the private key holder. These functions are not only useful when sending monetary transactions, but valuable for enterprises looking to participate in a blockchain consortium or network. Each participant can be validated, and certain data made visible only to certain recipients.

In an enterprise context, some blockchain frameworks will also support distribution of public keys within digital certificates, which are digital documents holding specific attributes along with the participant's public key. These certificates can be held by a trusted certificate authority (CA), which is also part of, or referenced by, the blockchain framework. Astute readers will immediately recognize that this places a reliance on a centralized component or trusted third party, which will definitely be an issue for blockchain purists and cause experienced technology architects to cringe. Building a distributed, decentralized system with a dependency on a single or centralized component is typically not a good idea.

Of course, hashing, private data, and public key cryptography are not the only topics related to blockchain security. Multi-party computing, confidential computing, and multi-signature schemes are also relevant, some of which are discussed in Chapter 9.

DISTRIBUTED NETWORK OF PARTICIPANTS

From our blockchain definition, "distribution" is closely related to the concept of decentralization described previously in this chapter.

From a technical standpoint, blockchain networks are distributed, with nodes running on machines typically not owned by any one organization. These nodes are the processing engines powering the blockchain network and performing various operations such as transaction verification, storage, data synchronization, and smart contract execution. With blockchain, the nodes represent and are owned by multiple parties. (A blockchain with two participants is *not* a good idea.)

It is also important to remember that the characteristics of a distributed system still apply in the blockchain world. The system must accommodate node failure and address issues such as fault tolerance, Byzantine faults, scalability, eventual consistency, and transparency. Despite the hype in previous years, blockchain does not circumvent the need for following distributed design and execution best practices. The laws of physics (and IT) still apply.

EMBEDDED BUSINESS LOGIC

The ability to embed business logic in a blockchain network is key to its use in the enterprise. Whether streamlining the exchange of information between participants, validating proposed changes to the underlying blockchain ledger, or automating the execution of business transactions, the ability to include some form of programmability in the network is an important function for enterprise deployments. Even the Bitcoin network includes business logic for transaction processing, although this logic, written in a language called Script, has limited functionality and is typically not used in an enterprise context.

In the blockchain world, this embedded logic is referred to as a smart contract. Smart contracts drive the business needs of the network and can be thought of as code that controls how changes are made to the blockchain in a non-centralized and potentially untrustworthy environment. The code is open, distributed, transparent, and runs on the blockchain nodes. It can be built using a variety of standard and proprietary languages including common programming languages such as Java and Golang or platform-specific languages such as Solidity.

We will cover smart contracts in Chapter 6, including a discussion of related challenges, and whether smart contracts are actually smart or contracts. For now, think of smart contracts as the application logic embedded within a blockchain network, whether for the purposes of building decentralized applications (dApps), facilitating decentralized finance (DeFi) or the exchange of NFTs, or supporting an improved way of implementing B2B-style capabilities in a network.

TRUST AND CONSENSUS

The final topic from our definition is the notion of trust, a characteristic typically associated with blockchain networks. Trust, including of humans and technical elements, is a broad topic. Its presence or lack in people, organizations, governments, and regulations are drivers behind many advancements in the blockchain space and the movement towards digital forms of currency.

You may have heard, for example, that blockchain allows trust to be brought to a trustless environment, but this is not completely accurate. Yes, a network like Bitcoin removes the need for certain third parties to participate in transaction processing, but you still need to trust the overall system, including the operation of the code, the miners and the hardware on which they run, the protocols, and the people governing the network. Thus, the system provides trust minimization, but is not without the need for trust, and in some use cases, the trust needed is greater or comes at a higher risk than if the network was not used at all.

Regardless, trust is important when building blockchain networks. Given our focus on the enterprise, when we refer to trust, we mean trust in the known participants, that each will behave in a manner supporting the overall health and well-being of the network, and that any data or information shared is secure, relevant, and accurate. As discussed previously, to support this trust, enterprise blockchain deployments will use capabilities such as the specialized form of DLT, public key cryptography, consensus, and smart contracts. These elements provide tamper-resistant, cryptographically linked shared storage, broad agreement, and transparent business logic so each participant can verify the network is working as expected. This doesn't remove the need to trust the underlying technology, nor does it eliminate the human element. It does, however, serve to support the level of trust necessary for the network to operate.

We are still missing the details behind one critical piece of the puzzle: consensus. In a distributed or multi-node system, it is important for each node to agree on the state of the network and ensure all copies of the underlying blockchain DLT are identical. Otherwise, if nodes have different views, the system quickly falls apart. The network needs a consistent view in the event of node failures, and the ability to handle a "bad actor" or malicious node.

With blockchain, the ability for distributed nodes to agree on the state of transactions is achieved through the use of consensus algorithms. This concept is not new, with approaches such as Byzantine Fault Tolerance (BFT), Practical Byzantine Fault Tolerance (PBFT), Paxos, and Raft used for years to solve problems associated with distributed shared state. You may have also heard of Proof of Work, the consensus algorithm used by the Bitcoin network to reach agreement on transactions to be added to the ledger. However, this is not the only algorithm used by blockchain networks, and in enterprise use cases, consensus may not only support the distribution of state but also the governance of the network. More on this topic in Chapter 7, but consensus, along with an understanding of the boundaries of trust, is part of what enables blockchain to function in an enterprise context.

OTHER KEY TERMS AND CONCEPTS

At this point, we have developed a more detailed understanding of the concepts behind our definition. But I am not quite done yet! There are a few other terms and concepts relevant to the enterprise, some of which are covered next.

Oracles

In many cases, it's necessary for a blockchain to access data originating from outside the network. For example, as part of its processing logic, a smart contract may need to reference external data—possibly from enterprise systems, APIs, cloud services, or other data providers. With traditional applications, accessing this information is straightforward. Technologies including APIs can expose data contained within trusted and secure enterprise systems and from known endpoints or providers. But how do you achieve this same capability in a blockchain with multiple participants, distributed nodes, and multiple smart contracts that need to access and agree on trusted, consistent, and externally provided data?

This is the role of an oracle. Oracles provide data to blockchain networks in a manner that matches the characteristics of the networks, including the need for external data to be tamper-resistant, trusted, and provided consistently to all nodes needing that data. Consider a simple situation where temperature data is needed by a smart contract. If the source of this data cannot be trusted, or if each blockchain node retrieves a different value as part of the same transaction, the network will either make decisions based on incorrect data or not reach consensus.

In certain permissioned deployments, it may be possible for participants to trust a single or centralized data source so that traditional data retrieval techniques are sufficient. But when this is not possible, or to reduce dependencies on centralized data sources, moving to a decentralized, oracle-based model is necessary.

Many forms of oracles exist, including software, hardware, or a consensus/quorum; successful use depends on oracle accuracy and trustworthiness. Oracles also typically push data into a blockchain network where it can be referenced by smart contracts as required, which is different from the pull model found in most applications. In a distributed system where processing does not occur simultaneously, having external data available on-chain eliminates the need for each smart contract to pull its data, and ensures the data is readily available, consistent, and verified across the network.

Zero-Knowledge Proofs

Storing data on a blockchain is tricky. Because blockchains store data in an append-only replicated data structure that is shared and potentially visible by all participants, the ability to store sensitive data such as financial records, contractual agreements, and medical information is limited. Furthermore, privacy regulations such as

GDPR add to this limitation because the right to be forgotten can be challenging to support in a data store with no delete or update functionality.

This behavior is both a strength and a weakness. In the enterprise, proving the validity and provenance of data is important, but many associated applications require some form of privacy for sharing data with a select group or for storing sensitive information. In a decentralized network, how can this seemingly opposing need for both privacy and auditability be accommodated?

Enter zero-knowledge proofs, or ZKPs. With ZKPs, sensitive data is not placed on the blockchain. Instead, a commitment is written to the ledger along with a proof validating the committed data. The commitment is a representation of the data, often generated through a hash function. The ZKP allows a party to verify data integrity without actually seeing it. The data remains private, but a participant with rights to the ledger can ensure the data is valid.

If this sounds like proving you've found Waldo[18] without actually showing anyone his location, you are absolutely right! But balancing privacy with the need to share and validate data is a key consideration for enterprises looking to adopt blockchain technology.

---

[18] Wikipedia, s.v. "Where's Wally?" last modified May 30, 2022, 05:15 (UTC), https://en.wikipedia.org/wiki/Where%27s_Wally%3F.

Zero-knowledge proofs represent one possible solution, which we will investigate further in Chapter 9.

Sidechains

For all the organic and biochemistry enthusiasts reading this book (!), the concept of a sidechain will be familiar. But instead of referencing proteins, in a blockchain, a sidechain is a secondary chain connected to the main chain. Designed to address issues such as performance and privacy, sidechains exchange assets among themselves and the main blockchain using constructs referred to as two-way pegs. These pegs allow assets to be exchanged at a predetermined rate, both from the main blockchain to the sidechain, and from the sidechain back to the main blockchain. Sidechains operate independently, may use their own protocols or consensus mechanisms, and may add or allow for testing new features and updates to the main blockchain. Currently used primarily in cryptocurrency use cases, sidechains offer promise for improved performance, security, and future blockchain interoperability.

Tokens

At a high level, a token is a digital representation of an asset. It may represent an entire asset, or a portion of an asset in situations where more than one party owns the asset. The rules or logic governing tokens are achieved through smart contracts, and supporting applications are typically built and deployed on a blockchain network.

A piece of expensive equipment, for example, could be fractionally owned by multiple parties, with the degree of ownership represented through corresponding tokens. Energy systems, such as distributed energy resources or DERs, are another opportunity for tokenization. Energy generation via assets such as solar panels or wind farms could again be represented and traded as tokens. Tokens represent a large potential opportunity for enterprises, and are discussed further in Chapter 11.

Decentralized Identity

Decentralized identity, otherwise referred to as self-sovereign identity (SSI), is a use case commonly discussed in blockchain circles. We dive into this topic in Chapter 8, but, in short, SSI is concerned with increasing the trust and security of one's identity and placing control of any associated data in the hands of the identity owner. Instead of freely giving one's identity information directly to a third party, or to an identity provider (IDP) such as Google or Facebook, a type of digital wallet containing verified credentials can be used to establish trust between the identity owner and another party. As much or as little of one's identity may be shared as needed, and the shared identity can be revoked by its owner at any time.

This is very different than what occurs today, where multiple usernames/passwords are needed, personal data is stored with multiple organizations, and identity data thefts are common. The problem of identity is not just associated with people or organizations. For example, as previously mentioned, IoT devices need verifiable identity so parties can be sure information generated and sent to one or more recipients is trustworthy. Many functions in finance, healthcare, government, and other areas are also heavily dependent on identity, making this a high-priority concern for the enterprise.

FINAL THOUGHTS

This chapter introduces many core concepts related to enterprise blockchains. I have introduced common terms—not every possible blockchain buzzword or acronym—with the goal of providing relevant context and background.

Merkle trees, forks, wallets, sybil attacks, DDOS attacks, state channels, DAO, and ERC20 are just some of the terms that will appear as you dig through this topic. The internet is your friend here, but be prepared to find strong, diverse opinions, variations in definitions, and lots of content on the "crypto" side of blockchain. For now, the content in this chapter should get you started and provide a foundation for understanding the rest of this book.

Chapter 4

BLOCKCHAIN MYTHS AND MISCONCEPTIONS

Blockchain has seen hype, excitement, and disillusionment. Whether caused by the price of Bitcoin or overzealous marketing departments, it has been associated with many promises and a seemingly endless supply of capabilities.

How much of the hype is real? Does blockchain really eliminate the need for third parties? Is data stored on a blockchain actually immutable? And what should an organization consider before adopting it? All great questions! And a great introduction to this chapter on myths, misconceptions, and organizational challenges to consider when investigating blockchain use.

"DECENTRALIZED WITH NO THIRD PARTY"

As discussed in previous chapters, one of the main characteristics used to describe blockchain is its ability to support transactions without needing a centralized third party. Networks such as Bitcoin are examples; no one entity controls the network. The Bitcoin network is self-contained, and governance and ownership are built into it. There's no third party to get in the way, leading to lower costs, improved transparency, and trust for the types of transactions supported.

These are common claims, but as noted in Chapter 1, it is very difficult to eliminate all third parties from the enterprise functions performed with a blockchain. Organizations do not operate in a vacuum. They are dependent on third parties and need to integrate with systems, devices, people, and other organizations outside of a blockchain context. Furthermore, enterprises may require a third party to run blockchain nodes, govern the network, and manage the relationships, legal or otherwise, within a blockchain consortium.

Even with networks such as Bitcoin and Ethereum, the level of decentralization or lack of third-party influence is not as great as you might think. Mining power is concentrated among relatively few miners or mining pools. Many blockchain nodes are located in common data centers, and decisions on the underlying network or code are made by a relatively small number of people. Yes, the network must come to consensus on any changes to the protocol (or force what's called a fork, which is a split in the network), but with public blockchains, miners control which blockchain they support. Emerging regulations and laws also threaten the level of decentralization currently provided by public blockchains.

With enterprise blockchains, it is not accurate to say the network can be completely decentralized or that it won't require third parties. The degree of centralization, and the number of third parties, can be reduced, but not eliminated, by using a blockchain framework.

"BLOCKCHAIN ENSURES DATA PRIVACY"

Other common blockchain misconceptions surround data privacy, data security, and data accuracy. Conventional wisdom has it that data stored on a blockchain is accurate, private, and secure, but in reality, the degree to which this can be achieved ranges from "not at all" to "probably."

First, data stored on a blockchain is only as good as its source. If bad data is submitted to the network, and controls such as smart contracts or other verification techniques are not in place, the network will distribute that inaccurate data to all relevant nodes. It will ensure the data is identical across those nodes, and cannot be easily changed or tampered with, but by default, it does nothing to verify data accuracy.

The use of trusted data sources, or oracles, can improve data accuracy, as can smart contracts or other data preparation techniques.

In an enterprise deployment, it is also less likely for participants to purposely submit inaccurate data, but obviously mistakes and differing views of data or state can occur. It is important to recognize that in the case of enterprise blockchain deployments, it is not safe to assume the data is completely accurate.

Second, data added to the network is not necessarily encrypted or private. The ability and extent to which protections can take effect differ by enterprise blockchain framework. It is not correct to assume data stored in a blockchain is completely safe, secure, and only viewable by certain participants. By default, data is often not encrypted, all participants have visibility into the entire ledger, any submitted transactions are visible by everyone, and the smart contract code supporting the network is completely transparent.

For permissioned use cases, privacy, security, and accuracy are addressed to varying degrees, and you must ensure the mechanisms for upholding each are used, correctly configured, and governed. Participants in the consortium must review the use of public key cryptography, ensure appropriately managed network access, and establish strict data governance rules over the data stored and shared. These measures include safely recording private keys, verifying the owner of these keys, and using appropriate cryptographic algorithms to ensure keys are generated and maintained without exposing vulnerabilities. Data sharing procedures also need to be reviewed to handle scenarios where participants should only see certain data elements to prevent information leaks.

Remember that the security of the network will only be as good as the underlying technology. If software bugs are prevalent, no amount of configuration or governance will be able to compensate. This not only applies to obvious network functions, but also to more obscure components such as the compiler behind the network's smart contract capabilities. Blockchain security is extremely important, with further details provided in Chapter 9.

"IMMUTABLE RECORD OF EVENTS"

Data stored in a blockchain network is often described as immutable. Because cryptographic hashing is used to create a chain of transactions, append operations are the only ones supported, and attempts to break this chain are detectable, the data must be immutable. At least, that is the perception, but is it true?

There are actually a number of gotchas, triggered by the implications of having an "immutable" data structure when humans are involved and mistakes or malicious acts are possible. For our purposes, we will break the concept of immutability into two parts: the technical characteristics and the implications of immutability, especially with enterprise blockchains. (I can feel the purists who have made it this far shudder!) Even though this is a sensitive topic, part of the goal of this book is to cover the concepts, make you aware of the issues, and discuss the trade-offs associated with the technology.

In Chapter 3, I introduced the blockchain DLT. Blocks of transactions are cryptographically linked to form a chain, and attempts to change these blocks can be detected given the nature of the chain of hashes. Blocks can only be added, and the ledger is replicated to each node on the network. This behavior, however, is not enough to ensure immutability. Consensus is also needed because each node must agree on the changes to be written. Once the validity, order, and timestamp of the transactions are agreed upon, the content is recorded.

Arguably, these operations only make the ledger tamper-resistant. True immutability implies the ledger never changes once established. However, history has shown, even in a public blockchain, that it is possible to "go back in time" and change or restore blockchain records. The historic hack in 2016 of the Ethereum public network is one example. A critical security flaw allowed a hacker to drain Ether (ETH), the public Ethereum network's native token. After much debate and controversy, it was decided to issue a hard fork, or blockchain protocol change, to reverse the theft. The end result was two blockchain networks, now known as Ethereum and Ethereum Classic. Philosophical differences aside, does this fork imply that under certain circumstances, a blockchain can be changed? Many say yes, making blockchain only tamper-resistant, not immutable.

Furthermore, going back to our blockchain structure, we know that attempting to change or inject a block into the chain will break the hashes and lead to detection of the hack. But what if an attacker, or group of attackers, could take over a network, and effectively recompute the chain of hashes from the beginning? Or, in the case of a public blockchain like Bitcoin, take over 51% of the network? This latter case would be very hard to achieve, of course, but still technically possible. It would, in essence, change the ledger and obviously break the immutability of the blockchain. Difficult to do, but not inconceivable, especially in a poorly implemented enterprise configuration or a relatively new deployment with few blocks on the ledger.

Lastly, enterprise blockchains operate in an environment involving external entities, including people, systems, and devices. As a result, mistakes can be made, and data can be added that is inaccurate, violates regulations, or furthers malicious behavior. Of course, various checks could be implemented to validate all input, and the governance model should define how to address or compensate for mistakes, but it is still possible for a blockchain to contain bad data. This has led to discussions on techniques for allowing data to be redacted from a blockchain, including the use of chameleon hashes, mutation via versioning, and mutation via voting. Accenture, for example, describes the use of chameleon hashes[19] to

---

[19] Richard Lumb, David Treat, and Owen Jelf, "Editing the Uneditable Blockchain: Why Distributed Ledger Technology Must Adapt to an Imperfect World," Accenture, 2016, https://newsroom.accenture.com/content/1101/files/Cross-FSBC.pdf.

support blockchain edits, as do approaches such as μchain[20] and permissionless blockchain redaction protocols.[21]

So blockchain, really, is not truly immutable. It comes down to the degree that immutability can be supported and associated trade-offs.

ENTERPRISE CHALLENGES AND CONSIDERATIONS

Beyond the misconceptions described in this chapter, enterprises face additional challenges, both technical and non-technical. I go into greater detail in Chapter 10, but some examples include:

- **The need for strong governance and stewardship.** Deploying a blockchain framework is only one piece of the puzzle. How will participants be verified and approved? By what process will participants join the network and under what guidelines? How will organizations leave the network either willingly or unwillingly? How will disputes be settled? What rules and regulations will govern the network? What incentives or penalties will ensure the network operates fairly? These are just a few of the questions to consider when creating a blockchain network.

---

[20] Ivan Puddu, Alexandra Dmitrienko, and Srdjan Capkun, "μchain: How to Forget without Hard Forks," Cryptology ePrint Archive, Report 2017/106, February 10, 2017, https://eprint.iacr.org/2017/106.

[21] Dominic Deuber et al., "Redactable Blockchain in the Permissionless Setting," in *2019 IEEE Symposium on Security and Privacy (SP 2019)*, (San Francisco, CA, 2019), 645–59. https://doi.org/10.48550/arXiv.1901.03206.

- And in many cases, bringing together diverse organizations that may actually compete in certain areas and getting them to agree on the rules by which the network will operate could be more complex and time-consuming than the technical deployment. This complexity is one of the reasons you will often see a press release announcing the formation of a consortium, or the selection of a blockchain framework by the consortium, but no further news or activity on a production deployment for months or even years.

- **Legal and regulatory risks.** Given the involvement of multiple organizations in a blockchain network, the subsequent legal agreements, and the government regulations applied to various types of business transactions, there is a need to ensure the network is complying with all required obligations. This compliance can be quite difficult to achieve because the participating organizations may span geographical and legal boundaries. Rules governing privacy, personally identifiable information (PII), and monetary and other factors often lag the "ingenuity" or functionality of the networks, and disputes may take time to resolve. If a new law is suddenly introduced, or an existing regulation is altered, it can negatively impact the operation of the network and even cause it to shut down. Risks are present in any vertical, but especially prominent in finance and healthcare, given the highly regulated nature of and sensitive data managed by these industries.

- **Operational complexity.** Operating a decentralized, distributed technology within one organization is difficult,
  never mind multiple organizations. Implementation details
  aside, the participants need to agree on the operation of the
  network. How will the system be upgraded? What type of
  management and monitoring will be established? Who will
  operate the different types of nodes in a typical enterprise
  deployment? How will the network be supported? How
  will revenue be calculated and distributed? As with any
  solution, developing a proof-of-concept is the simple part.
  Moving the solution to production and ensuring it operates
  smoothly is much more difficult.

- **The challenge of picking a winner.** Most organizations
  can't afford to constantly rewrite a deployed application.
  Solutions have an associated business value often recognized over years. With today's emerging and rapidly evolving approaches to enterprise blockchain technology and
  associated frameworks, how do you pick a winner? Which
  framework will meet the needs of the network now and in
  the future? I examine sample selection criteria later in this
  book, but the pace of technology change and blockchain's
  use in the midst of evolving regulations makes this challenge a moving target.

Furthermore, if it is determined that a blockchain solution is appropriate for a particular business problem, this solution will not

operate in a vacuum. Organizations have systems, processes, and data, and each must be considered in the context of a blockchain solution. For example, organizations must decide:

- **How to get data in or out of a blockchain.** As discussed, an enterprise blockchain network needs to exchange data with outside systems. How will this integration be established? What security mechanisms will be used? How much data, and at what rate? How will data consistency and integrity be maintained?

- **How to extend smart contract logic to the enterprise.** Smart contracts drive the business logic in the network, but represent only a small fraction of the logic driving an organization. What logic should be included in the network versus executed outside it? What level of transparency is desired for smart contracts? How often will this logic change? How will this logic be kept consistent with the rest of the organization?

- **How to respond to events from the ledger.** Today, organizations are focused on becoming real-time and event-driven, with business decisions made immediately in response to key opportunities or threats. It is not efficient to continuously poll a system for transactions of interest (which may not be present at the time of the poll), nor can organizations wait to process key transactions as part of a batch process.

Ledger transactions can be critical to the functioning of an organization, so it is important that they either initiate business functions as soon as they are available or enter the network as soon as certain conditions are met. How will these events be generated? Are the off-chain systems capable of receiving blockchain events?

- **How to analyze data contained within the ledger.** Data and analytics are critical components of any organization. However, the data structures supporting blockchain are not optimized for in-depth analytical operations, and all of the data needed for these models is likely not present on the blockchain. Is copying this data to a separate, off-chain datastore more appropriate for analytical processing? How will the integrity of the off-chain data be maintained with the on-chain data?

- **How to provide controlled, managed access to blockchain capabilities.** As mentioned, security is a key consideration for blockchain deployments. In addition to the matters discussed, it is also necessary to review how access to the blockchain functions will be managed. Who within an organization will have access to the blockchain APIs? What security model will be used to invoke these APIs? Are the APIs request-response or are event-driven APIs supported?

It is important to address all these points, or the value of a block-chain solution can be lost and the system will simply become too complex. With distributed, decentralized applications, development may also be slower due to the implications of making a mistake, as more than one organization is affected. Changes need to be agreed upon by various participants, overall maintenance can be challenging, and performance can be a concern. Decentralization comes at a cost, and it is important to consider these costs when determining if a blockchain solution is appropriate.

FINAL THOUGHTS

From this discussion, it is obvious that the world of blockchain can be very confusing. Myths and misconceptions still circulate, and the complexities of building a decentralized, distributed network can be vast. It can also be challenging to distinguish between public blockchains and permissioned enterprise networks, which will either get more (or less) confusing as the lines between these concepts continue to blur. However, for the reasons described in Chapter 1, blockchain still has relevance for the enterprise, which we continue to investigate in the remaining chapters. Don't believe the hype, but go below the surface and break through the misconceptions—familiar recommendations for anyone diving into a new technology, and definitely applicable to blockchain.

Chapter 5

BLOCKCHAIN, DLT, OR SOMETHING ELSE?

In Chapter 3, I introduced distributed ledgers and their relationship to blockchain, but only scratched the surface of blockchain storage. In reality, many variations exist, and entire technology stacks have emerged to try and solve the problems associated with building a distributed, secure, and peer-to-peer data management capability.

This chapter takes a deeper look at these technologies and reviews the characteristics of several common ledger storage technologies. Don't think of this as a review of all possible choices; there are many! Instead, I select a few that are typically encountered and discuss whether the commonly used blockchain descriptors—"immutable" and "append-only"—are actually desired traits of permissioned or enterprise implementations. It's a controversial subject I highlighted in the previous chapter, and one worth exploring further.

DISTRIBUTED LEDGER TECHNOLOGY (DLT)

To start, let's review what's meant by a DLT and how it relates to blockchain. First, distributed ledger technology is not new; the technology has been around for many years but has experienced a resurgence given the interest in blockchain. Second, by itself, a DLT may be simply thought of as a decentralized, distributed database where data is replicated across several nodes, there is no single point of failure or control, and specific protocols and algorithms are used to ensure each node agrees on the current state of the system, even in the event of node failures or malicious action. Third, while a blockchain is a form of DLT, not every DLT is a blockchain. Blockchain underpins a DLT and provides the mechanisms by which "blocks" or transactions are bundled into data structures, cryptographically linked, and subsequently distributed to required nodes via the DLT and its consensus algorithm.

Consensus, of course, is a key aspect of DLT, blockchain frameworks, and distributed systems. It's through consensus that the network achieves an agreed-upon state, regardless of whether it's public, permissioned, or based on blockchain or non-blockchain data structures. Given the importance of consensus, it's more thoroughly addressed in Chapter 7. For now, it's good enough to know that consensus algorithms such as Proof of Work, Proof of Stake, Practical Byzantine Fault Tolerance (PBFT), and many others all have their own characteristics and behavior. The algorithm used, in addition to allowing the DLT to function properly, differentiates the framework. And, in an attempt to solve problems of performance, high availability/fault tolerance (HA/FT), privacy, and others, a substantial amount of effort and research is spent on DLT algorithms, so expect continued advancements and innovation in this area.

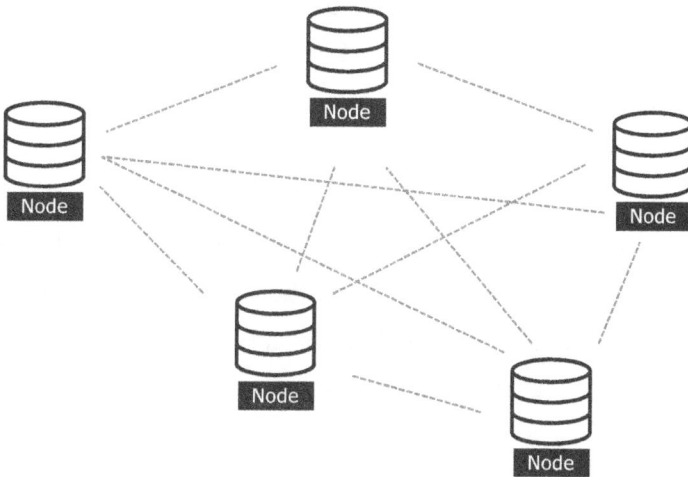

Network of nodes, with no central party, each with their own copy of data

As an aside, note that not every blockchain technology organizes transactions into "blocks." In some cases, given the targeted nature of transaction delivery in permissioned enterprise blockchain networks, it doesn't make sense to insert unrelated transactions into a block because not every transaction may be destined for every node or participant. Thus, some approaches will order and cryptographically link individual transactions, and then allow the DLT to handle the distribution of these related transactions to all required nodes.

On-Chain or Off-Chain?

One of the key challenges when deploying a DLT or blockchain solution has to do with data management. What data should be stored on-chain (in the DLT) versus off-chain (in a separate data store)? How much data should be stored? Which participant needs to see which data records? Because the data cannot be easily deleted or updated, what data can be stored "forever"? How will mistakes or inaccurate data be handled? What data privacy regulations need to be considered?

The answers to these questions are critical to a successful enterprise DLT or blockchain implementation. Remember, the distributed, decentralized nature of these systems makes replicating large amounts of data very challenging. Data transfer speed is a concern because the speed at which data is sent or received will be affected by various factors, including the performance of the physical network and the capabilities of the nodes. Also, remember that the system will only become consistent eventually; data in a distributed system doesn't arrive simultaneously (or at all) at every node, and its delivery will be affected by node and other infrastructure failures. These realities result in a potentially complex deployment. And they are also one of the reasons why organizations need to carefully study whether a DLT or blockchain is required for their use case, or if an alternate data storage mechanism is sufficient.

Regardless of whether a DLT or blockchain approach is used, there are techniques available to help address the aforementioned data management problems. For example, sensitive data can be stored off-chain with techniques such as zero-knowledge proofs (ZKPs) that allow other nodes to verify the validity of the data on the ledger. We discuss ZKPs further in Chapter 9, but as mentioned earlier, they allow participants to verify the integrity of data without actually seeing the data.

Public key cryptography can be used to encrypt data elements so the data is only accessible by participants with the proper keys. And hashes, computed against external data, can be stored on the ledger to provide a unique fingerprint of the data for later verification. In addition, certain blockchain frameworks allow data to be shared only with certain participants over constructs typically referred to as "channels." Participants with the proper access privileges can use these channels to share data not available to any other party. However, this point-to-point data distribution may result in an additional layer of system complexity, especially if you need to configure and maintain direct channels for large numbers of participants.

Analytics also figures into the on-chain versus off-chain decision. DLTs or blockchains can hold and reference valuable data for analytical processes and models, but accessing this data presents challenges. Ledger data structures are not optimized for large-scale analytical processing, and the relatively limited storage capacity of the ledger means that a portion of the data needed for analysis will often be stored in an off-chain location. You can replicate ledger data into a more appropriate data store, but this can result in data that is centralized and disconnected from the data in the DLT. Alternatively, hashes could be used to create links back to the analytical datasets, but verifying these hashes when data is read or processed can negatively impact performance. Unfortunately, there is no "one-size-fits-all" solution, especially when requirements related to privacy, auditability, and security are added to the equation.

Is Immutability Desired?

One inevitable (and often hotly debated) question related to data management and permissioned networks involves asking whether the "immutability" property, or rather the "tamper-resistant" property as discussed in Chapter 4, is desired in all cases. In certain circumstances, the answer is straightforward. For example, it's best to have key financial transactions adhere to this property. But for other types of transactions, some form of mutation may be acceptable, although this obviously goes against all purist notions of what a blockchain is. However, realistically, given human mistakes, changing regulations, GDPR, and evolving use cases, it is important to consider the question, especially if you expect the adoption of blockchain networks to increase, and the technology to appropriately evolve.

Accenture, for example, has published research[22] describing possible options for supporting blockchain edits in enterprise deployments.

---

[22] David Treat, "Editing the Uneditable," Accenture, https://www.accenture.com/ca-en/insight-editing-uneditable-blockchain.

More details are provided in the publication, but essentially the approaches involve editing or removing blocks of data without breaking the chain, updating flawed smart contracts, and doing so while ensuring the change itself is recorded and unable to be removed. The need for hard forks, or essentially a new chain, is eliminated, and there is no need to rebuild blocks after the block change. This option does, however, require strong governance and guidelines to control the conditions under which a change could occur. Subsequently, it is mostly applicable in a permissioned blockchain context.

Other research on immutability includes the use of chameleon hashes and "trapdoor" keys, or supporting multiple versions of a transaction with a corresponding mutation policy. (See https://eprint.iacr.org/2017/106.pdf for an example.) In this research, key characteristics of blockchain, such as enforcement through consensus and verifiable transactions, are maintained. Regardless of whether these techniques are employed, it is important to understand the true meaning of "immutability" in a blockchain system and the implications of working with a distributed, append-only data structure.

ALTERNATIVE STORAGE

Amongst the distributed ledger technology (DLT) underpinning many common blockchain frameworks, a separate category of storage has emerged. It attempts to retain certain characteristics of a DLT while eliminating others or provide data structures beyond a sequence of cryptographically linked blocks. This book doesn't cover all possible variations of these storage mechanisms, but does present examples commonly found in enterprise blockchain discussions.

Ledger Databases

In many use cases, a decentralized, distributed blockchain network with embedded consensus and smart contracts is not required. Instead, what is needed is simply an auditable data trail where stored data can be cryptographically verified as not having been tampered with or changed. It is also acceptable to have this audit trail owned by a central party and access for other participants granted by this central party.

To meet this requirement, many software companies are promoting what are typically referred to as ledger databases. A relatively immature technology, ledger databases provide some of the benefits of a blockchain framework without many of the complexities. The technology itself is owned, run, governed, and managed by a central organization and offers increased performance because there is no need for network-wide consensus or data replication for each network participant. It provides support for storing data in a tamper-resistant audit trail, which is created through the use of hashing and cryptographic techniques much like blockchain. However, it does place control in the hands of a single organization, which can be a concern for use cases requiring broader agreement, trust, transparency, and embedded business logic.

Ledger databases do not meet all the requirements of a blockchain network, but for use cases requiring support for auditing, data lineage, or data tracking, they can be great options. Following are examples of ledger database technologies in the market at the time of this writing. These technologies will likely evolve and new players emerge.

Amazon QLDB

Amazon is one of the large software vendors providing ledger database technology with its Quantum Ledger Database (https://aws .amazon.com/qldb/). Offered as a fully managed service on AWS, QLDB provides a "transparent, immutable, and cryptographically verifiable transaction log owned by a central trusted authority." This functionality is supported through the use of immutable, append-only journals materialized in the form of tables to the user.

Oracle Blockchain Tables

Oracle, a traditional database and application vendor, has also announced support for a tamper-resistant ledger as part of its Oracle database technology stack (https://docs.oracle.com/en/data base/oracle/oracle-database/21/nfcon/oracle-blockchain-table -268779556.html). At a high level, the Oracle Blockchain Table provides functionality similar to Amazon's QLDB, allowing cryptographically verifiable chains of records to be created when storing data. However, the implementation is somewhat different from

AWS in that it's based on database tables and organizing rows into one or more chains within these tables.

Fluree

Amongst other capabilities, Fluree (https://flur.ee/) can be used as a form of ledger database with the ability to augment the database with query, semantic graph, distributed deployment, consensus via RAFT, and business rule functionality.

Gospel Data Platform

The Gospel Data Platform (https://gospel.tech/) is also a form of a ledger database and can be used to form a private, permissioned distributed ledger. Consensus is supported for both reads and writes. Data access is logged in a tamper-proof audit trail, and notifications and triggers are supported.

Other options, such as OrbitDB (https://orbitdb.org/) and BigChainDB (https://www.bigchaindb.com/), are also possibilities for organizations researching the use of ledger databases within their environment.

IPFS

The InterPlanetary File System (https://ipfs.io/), although not specifically a blockchain, DLT, or ledger database, is another distributed storage system commonly discussed in blockchain circles. In short, IPFS is a "distributed system for storing and accessing files, websites, applications, and data." This sounds a lot like the internet as it exists today, but there are substantial differences. Instead of pointing to content via its location, such as through the URL, https://en.wikipedia.org/wiki/InterPlanetary_File_System, IPFS cryptographically hashes the content, distributes it across many peers, and subsequently allows the content to be retrieved through the hash (content-based addressing). These capabilities allow users to retrieve content from more than one location, verify the content has not been changed (or else it would have a new hash), and ensure content is delivered from a nearby peer instead of potentially from across the globe.

Additional features include distributed hash tables for key-value mapping, Merkle DAGs (directed acyclic graphs) for content representation, and naming services for allowing content to be modified but still accessed via a specific address. In general, the goal of IPFS is to make content more accessible, resilient, and distributed, and to support creation of a decentralized web environment.

IPFS is also applicable to blockchain environments given the need as previously discussed to store certain amounts of data off-chain. With IPFS, it is possible to store a content hash on a blockchain, optionally control access to this hash or stored content via public key cryptography or smart contracts, and then use the hash to retrieve the content as needed via the IPFS network. This capability eliminates the need to store large amounts of content on the ledger, while still allowing the content to be accessed through resilient, decentralized storage.

Directed Acyclic Graphs

The final DLT-related approach covered here involves the use of directed acyclic graphs, or DAGs, along with specialized consensus protocols to create blockchain-inspired networks. Organizations such as Hedera (https://hedera.com/), with the Hedera Hashgraph public distributed ledger, and IOTA's Tangle (https://www.iota.org/), propose secure, peer-to-peer decentralized networks with data organized as graphs as opposed to a linear, cryptographically linked blockchain data structure.

The resulting networks are not based on blockchain, and given the newness of the technology, adoption is currently limited compared to blockchain-backed frameworks. However, DAGs promise advantages in performance, cost, transaction finality, and security, especially for public deployments, or deployments requiring zero-fee transactions such as the IoT.

Blockchain   (DAG/Directed Acyclic Graph)

Typical blockchain vs. directed acyclic graph structures

The implementation behind these networks is also somewhat different from what has been discussed so far. With Tangle, for example, each transaction is attached to two previous transactions, which forms a graph of transactions in the network. Transactions may be placed anywhere in the Tangle, miners are not used, and Proof of Work is used only to discourage spam transactions. Hashgraph, in comparison, uses a graph of hashes along with a gossip protocol and a virtual voting approach to reach agreement on transactions.

As mentioned, these technologies are relatively young, and so have limitations to be aware of. Tangle currently relies on a trusted, centralized "coordinator" to confirm transactions, while Hashgraph is governed by a group of term-limited enterprises. These limitations will likely be removed as the technology evolves, but at the time of this writing, they are factors to consider.

FINAL THOUGHTS

Distributed ledger technologies, or alternatives such as ledger databases, IPFS, and graph data structures, are the core foundation behind decentralized, distributed, and secure enterprise blockchain applications. I look at alternatives later in the book and further investigate the trade-offs between decentralized and centralized approaches. For now, it's important to understand the various storage options and how certain blockchain attributes and characteristics are or are not achieved. Next up, smart contracts!

Chapter 6

BLOCKCHAIN SMART CONTRACTS

Outside of its people, the heart of any enterprise is business logic. Business logic drives how data is created and shared, how processes are executed, and how applications provide the many functions needed to deliver goods and services. This logic can come in many forms, from COBOL in a mainframe environment to Go in a microservice, and is only limited by imagination and the laws of physics (plus silly things like budget or legal and regulatory requirements, of course). Without it, organizations could not function, and thus they spend a substantial amount of time, money, and effort refining and adjusting operations to drive desired outcomes.

To support business logic within a blockchain, certain frameworks let developers create what are commonly referred to as "smart contracts." Like many blockchain technologies, smart contracts are not new. Often attributed to computer scientist and cryptographer Nick

Szabo, smart contracts were first introduced in 1994 as "a set of promises, specified in digital form, including protocols within which the parties perform on these promises." Unlike paper-based equivalents, they are "smart" because they have the ability to automate certain programmed functions, and they are "contracts" to the extent that their code is recognized as law by the prevailing authorities.

In a blockchain network, smart contracts are the programs or code that invoke responses to transactions and handle changes in state for the purposes of streamlining participant interactions, tokenizing assets, exchanging cryptocurrency, providing financial services, or supporting any other blockchain application. Smart contracts are the embedded business logic of a blockchain solution and control how changes are made to the blockchain in a decentralized and potentially untrustworthy environment.

Sounds simple, but smart contracts have many nuances. This chapter delves into them and looks at some smart contract characteristics, considerations, best practices, and challenges. You may not be a smart contract developer, but it is important to understand the implications of this functionality as blockchain projects are evaluated, built, and deployed.

CHARACTERISTICS OF SMART CONTRACTS

You may have heard of smart contracts in the context of dApps, or decentralized applications built and commonly deployed on blockchain networks such as Ethereum. Decentralized finance (DeFi) applications are an example, as are several token-based systems and the currently popular non-fungible tokens (NFTs), further covered in Chapter 11. Decentralized applications may also be written to support various enterprise use cases, some of which I discussed in Chapter 2.

dApps consist of application and user interface code and are deployed alongside a blockchain network. They depend on smart contracts for back-end business logic, and these smart contracts are written using some form of a programming language. Smart contracts are typically deployed to all blockchain nodes participating in the consensus protocol, which means they are decentralized, distributed, and transparent. It also means that for each inbound transaction, all participating nodes run the identical smart contract in parallel, and each node needs to reach the same result or the transaction will be rejected. This parallelism promotes open, secure, and agreed-upon validation of both the code and the transaction, often at the cost of performance, scalability, and efficiency.

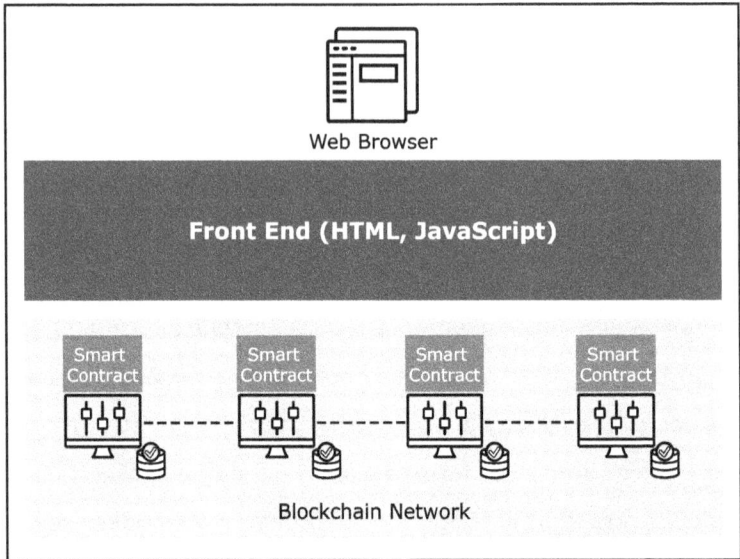

Simple decentralized application (dApp) architecture

In Ethereum, for example, smart contracts are primarily written in a proprietary language called Solidity, compiled to binary, and deployed via a blockchain transaction where they are loaded into Ethereum virtual machines (EVMs) by nodes across the network. However, Ethereum is not the only environment to support smart contracts. Hyperledger Fabric, R3 Corda, Kadena, Cosmos, and many other blockchain platforms offer smart contract capabilities. In some cases, such as in Ethereum, the contracts are defined as Turing complete. In theory, this allows developers to write code for any computational problem, although Ethereum does place restrictions on constructs such as recursion via its gas model (the fee required to execute a smart contract on its network). Alternatively, other frameworks may incorporate a smart contract language specific to an industry or use case to reduce the chance of errors and exploits. Smart contracts may exist as code only, or they may augment traditional text-based contracts when it is difficult to represent all contractual obligations and terms in code. It is also common for smart contracts to require access to external or off-chain data, which is best achieved through the use of oracles or other trusted sources as covered earlier in this book.

The decision on whether to use a general or application-specific smart contract language and blockchain environment is worth further mention. With general environments such as Ethereum, all smart contract code is run by a common runtime (the Ethereum virtual machine). Various dApps can co-exist on the same network, and capabilities such as the consensus protocol, cryptographic operations, and programming languages are fixed within the specific network deployment. This configuration may work well with certain use cases, such as exchanging assets represented as ERC-20 tokens on Ethereum, or creating unique ERC-721 non-fungible tokens, but this "one-size-fits-all" model does not work for many enterprise use cases.

For enterprises, it may be preferable to use an application-specific blockchain where the environment is assembled from a series of loosely coupled building blocks. Organizations select the smart contract language, consensus protocol, ledger structure, and security features most appropriate for their use case or application. In this scenario, an application has its own dedicated network, so that code issues do not impact other applications, and network features can be balanced against other requirements such as performance. This approach allows an organization to assemble the best collection of components for its application, but it also introduces the need to deploy multiple networks (one per application) and support information exchange among them.

Cosmos (https://cosmos.network/) and Polkadot (https://polka dot.network/) are two organizations working on the concept of application-specific blockchains. These projects aim to provide a framework for the "internet of blockchains" that will allow for seamless interoperability between blockchains, including environments such as Bitcoin and Ethereum. The ability to assemble networks from a series of building blocks, with the resulting deployment optimized for a specific use case, shows promise and could broaden the reach of blockchain in the enterprise. It is likely we will see more work in this area in the coming years.

Creating Smart Contracts

In many ways, creating dApps and smart contracts is similar to how enterprise developers create software applications. Select a framework; learn the APIs and libraries; choose appropriate development, testing, and automation tools; translate the desired business rules into code; test; and deploy the code into a runtime environment. Common programming languages, such as Java and Go, are supported by many blockchain frameworks, and many large cloud vendors offer blockchain-as-a-service (BaaS) tools and platforms. AWS, for example, offers both Hyperledger Fabric and Ethereum as part of its Amazon Managed Blockchain service, and IBM provides support for ledger services such as Hyperledger Fabric. These cloud BaaS environments streamline the installation and configuration of blockchain solutions, and provide additional cloud-based tools and management capabilities for application development.

However, as is common with blockchain, many associated complexities quickly make themselves apparent. First, the tools tend to be immature and usable only by those with deep programming skills. Environments such as Remix, Truffle, and Ganache simplify development for Ethereum dApps, but tools for other blockchain frameworks are often limited to those provided by the vendor, or to generic coding IDEs such as VS Code and other open-source tools. Second, as I cover later in this chapter, building a decentralized, distributed, secure, trusted, and multi-party network on a platform designed to prevent updates or deletes requires careful thought and knowledge of numerous computer science topics.

Additionally, with so many options for creating and using smart contracts, and so many blockchain technologies with varying support for this feature, it's difficult to create smart contracts that can be deployed across multiple platforms and integrated into the enterprise. A developer needs deep knowledge of each blockchain platform, sharing smart contracts is difficult, vendor lock-in is inevitable, and there's no such thing as moving logic between platforms; you need a complete rewrite. Open-source tools (such as Project Dovetail, https://www.tibco.com/solutions/blockchain) that strive to bring model-driven approaches to blockchain applications for rapid, standardized development of reusable smart contracts are only one part of the puzzle. A successful enterprise dApp deployment requires several architectural components, which I touch on in Chapter 10.

Securing Smart Contracts

Smart contracts do not have a history of being 100 percent secure and reliable. For example, in 2017, a bug in a particular smart contract resulted in the theft of over $30 million in ETH (Ethereum's token). This is not the only occurrence of theft, but it is certainly one of the best known. And while this is a public blockchain example, the impact of a bug or security vulnerability in a permissioned or consortium smart contract can be just as devastating.

Poorly written or untested code is one obvious source of security vulnerabilities, and there are many others. It is possible, for example, for a smart contract compiler to be an attack vector. How many people understand the inner workings of their compiler, and the instructions it generates? Malware could be present on the operating system of the machines running blockchain nodes, or a weak consensus protocol may allow for attacks against the network.

Further, the human element is not removed completely from the operations of the network, which may be another source of intrusion. To add to the complexity, all these attack surfaces are not confined to a single organization, but in varying forms are in all participating organizations. The network will only be as secure as the weakest link, and a breach in any of these areas could impact all participants.

In addition to thorough testing and code validation, other methods are available to address smart contract security concerns. Multi-signature (multisig) contracts can be created that require multiple keys, typically owned by multiple people or organizations, for approving and signing a transaction before it is executed. Verification techniques that prove the correctness of a smart contract by comparing its mathematical model to a formal specification are available for certain implementations. And the ability to run smart contracts in a trusted execution environment (TEE) is progressing. Security in blockchain networks is a very broad topic, one covered further in Chapter 9.

SMART CONTRACT CHALLENGES AND CONSIDERATIONS

As we have seen, creating and deploying smart contracts is not trivial. In addition to the items discussed previously, enterprises face a number of other considerations, including:

- **Infrastructure.** Smart contracts do not run in a vacuum; they require infrastructure in the form of hardware, networks, operating systems, and storage, along with connectivity to enterprise systems and each network participant. Decisions need to be made as to where each blockchain node will be installed, run, and managed. Will each participant configure and run their own infrastructure, which provides more flexibility and autonomy but is complex and expensive to maintain? Or will shared cloud services be used, which simplify the infrastructure but lead to increased centralization? Matters such as infrastructure consistency, patches, version upgrades, system availability, and failure recovery also need to be addressed to ensure the network and corresponding smart contracts are as resilient and performant as possible.

- **Collaboration.** Successful blockchain networks include more than one participant, so a certain level of collaboration, coordination, stewardship, and governance is needed among the parties. For example, how will coding errors be handled? How will consensus on business rules and transactions be achieved? How will changes be handled? For some of these considerations, it is possible to capture the governing rules in smart contracts, including the creation of automated voting processes for participant onboarding/ offboarding. However, given the current regulatory and legal climate under which enterprises operate, additional means of collaboration will be required.

- **Legal considerations.** The question of whether smart contracts are legal contracts is key. I am not a lawyer and can't
  speak from a legal point of view to provide a simple yes or no
  answer. However, current thinking on this question takes
  into account the type of contract, the legal jurisdiction, and
  whether the basic elements of a contract are found in the
  implementation. In some cases, the language associated
  with a contract may be fully captured in code; in others, it
  is likely the code will be augmented with traditional textual
  contracts. The former results in a less ambiguous contract
  because the elements are codified; the latter leaves room
  for interpretation by the courts. Given the challenges of
  determining smart contract enforceability, most permissioned or consortium blockchains will create a separate set
  of governing rules to cover areas such as participant roles
  and responsibilities, penalties for non-compliance, incentive
  models, and dispute resolution. As mentioned, the complexity behind these multi-party agreements can be greater than
  the technical delivery and is a common reason why many
  blockchain solutions never get beyond proof of concept.

- **Lack of standards.** Currently, there are no standards for
  smart contract development across blockchain platforms.
  Standards are defined within certain networks, but these
  are not widely shared. Between platforms, APIs vary
  greatly, different programming languages are supported,
  and smart contract operations are specific to a platform.

This incompatibility can result in vendor lock-in with limited portability if moving to a different blockchain platform is desired. To address this situation, some frameworks provide support for defining smart contracts that will run on multiple blockchain environments. Others offer a limited ability to mix smart contract types, such as running Ethereum smart contracts on Hyperledger Fabric through Hyperledger Burrow (https://www.hyperledger.org/use /hyperledger-burrow). The trade-off, however, is additional layers of complexity or third-party dependencies.

- **Programming errors and code upgrades.** Developing and deploying code into a decentralized, distributed system with multiple parties is challenging. Updating or redeploying a smart contract will require careful coordination, agreement of multiple parties, and a deep understanding of the impact to past, current, and future transactions. Each blockchain platform also supports contract upgrades differently, from the use of proxy contracts in Ethereum, to chaincode definition approvals, endorsement policies, and commits in Hyperledger Fabric. Thorough testing is critical, and techniques such as formal verification or mathematical proofs may be required. Also, the smart contract code will evolve over time, as will the code of the underlying blockchain framework. New features need to be carefully adopted and accommodated as needed, under the guidance of the rules governing the network.

- **Performance.** Enterprise blockchain networks are not widely known for supporting large-scale deployments with large numbers of transactions per second or vast amounts of data. Data replication, ledger data structures, complex logic, consensus protocols, multiple nodes, and other limitations all contribute to performance bottlenecks, further discussed in Chapter 10.

BEST PRACTICES FOR SMART CONTRACTS

Given these challenges, you may wonder how anyone could successfully deploy a smart contract! But it is possible, especially with the right planning and analysis. To assist, I have found it helpful to establish and document guiding principles and best practices at the beginning of any enterprise smart contract implementation. These principles guide development, establish coding practices and patterns, and govern deployments. The following represents a sample checklist of items to describe, which might need to be augmented for a specific use case or blockchain framework:

- **Data.** What data will be managed and stored by the smart contract on-chain vs. off-chain, and what data will be provided by oracles or other trusted external sources? Will the smart contract work with data references or hashes to off-chain data? How much state needs to be kept on-chain vs. off-chain?

With enterprise deployments, certain data elements may
be stored outside the blockchain ledger due to size constraints, cost, privacy laws, or other considerations. In this
case, a hash of the data, as well as a link or reference to the
external data, could be kept on the ledger. This hash may
then be used to ensure external data has not changed when
accessed by a smart contract. External storage requirements, however, do add additional complexity because
issues such as access, security, availability, and performance
need to be considered.

- **Business logic.** What business logic will be executed
  on-chain vs. off-chain? Will transactions be executed
  between parties over a sidechain or state channel,
  and subsequently settled to a main chain? I discuss
  sidechains and state channels later in the book, but in
  short, these solutions have been introduced as possible
  mechanisms for increasing performance in a blockchain
  environment.

- **Programming language.** What programming language(s)
  will be used? What patterns or language constructs need to
  be followed or omitted to ensure proper code behavior and
  determinism in the network (concurrency, read-after-write,
  parameter validation, use of loops, etc.)? What tools will
  be used to support development?

- **Encryption.** What data needs to be encrypted? Who can see what data? What testing or formal verification techniques will be used to verify smart contract logic?

- **Transactions.** What transactions are able to change the state of the ledger? Who can invoke what transaction? What is the expected rate of transactions, and does this match the capabilities of the selected blockchain framework?

- **Error handling.** How will error handling be performed? What procedures will be used to control access to the smart contract? What event mechanisms will be used to produce or receive smart contract events for enterprise systems?

- **Invocation and consensus.** What security processes will be used to control smart contract invocation? What consensus protocol will be used by the network?

- **Governance.** Do any governing principles impact smart contract design and implementation? What is the role of each participant in the network with regards to smart contract development, testing, approvals, and deployment? How will version changes or upgrades be agreed upon and synchronized? Has a formal lifecycle management process or workflow been defined?

This is not a complete list, but it does point out areas to consider when developing smart contracts for an enterprise blockchain network. In general, it is best to keep smart contracts as light as possible, test early, test often, and not burden the network with large amounts of data or complex processing requirements. Remember, different blockchain networks provide a different range of smart contract capabilities, and early identification of the business requirements for your solution will help in selecting the best blockchain technology.

FINAL THOUGHTS

Similar to applications and business logic captured in traditional software programs, the success of a smart contract depends on the developer, the framework behind the code, and the governance structures surrounding the deployment. In the end, smart contracts are code, and many of the best practices used during enterprise development projects still apply.

This takes us to the concept of consensus, one of the most critical and strongly debated aspects of blockchain. If you have wondered about phrases and terms such as Proof of Work, Proof of Stake, RAFT, PBFT, transaction finality, and settlement, then get ready for some fun!

Chapter 7

CONSENSUS AND TRANSACTION FINALITY

In Chapter 3, we introduced the importance of consensus in decentralized, distributed systems and the role it plays in blockchain. For blockchain networks to work, an agreed-upon, synchronized state of the system is needed, as is the ability to accommodate a loss or failure of a certain number of nodes. All this needs to be achieved securely without a central governing authority and in the possible presence of malicious actors.

Without consensus, a blockchain network could not operate. Nodes would have differing views of network state, transactions would not reach agreement or be added to the underlying ledger, and overall participant behavior could not be trusted. Such a flawed network would obviously fail, which is why consensus and transaction finality receive a lot of attention in the marketplace.

As I set out here, many methodologies and techniques are available in the market, with more regularly introduced and positioned as key differentiating features. This chapter provides the foundation needed to help identify the consensus and transaction finality methods best suited to your needs.

IT'S ALL ABOUT AGREEMENT

Consensus, whether in a permissioned or permissionless system, is a critical aspect of a blockchain. Consensus promotes trust and minimizes the need for trusted third parties to run the network. It ensures agreement on the order and validity of committed transactions, and does so in the presence of unreliable or even malicious components. It ensures all nodes, or at least those nodes deemed to be operating correctly, will:

- Decide on an output value or transaction ("termination")

- Agree on this value ("agreement")

- Handle all client requests and continue to add transactions ("liveness")

- Correctly execute requests in order ("safety")

These four conditions define consensus in distributed computing, and are fulfilled in different ways by consensus algorithms. Other terms may be used for these conditions, but in general, non-faulty nodes should produce values, values should be agreed upon, the system should not halt, and ordering should be respected.

To appreciate the challenge of providing these capabilities in today's technology environments, it's helpful to first take a step back and review a few of the complexities involved in building decentralized, distributed systems. Blockchain is a type of distributed system, and so the learnings from decades of research in this area of computer science also apply to blockchain deployments.

The subject of distributed systems is broad and includes many concepts and architectures. This chapter doesn't cover all aspects but reviews concepts closely related to blockchain and consensus. First, I highlight the key properties of a distributed system, describe different types of communications patterns, and discuss fault tolerance. I use a common computer science construct to describe state management, and then relate all this to blockchain and examples of real-world consensus algorithms.

It's also important to recognize that consensus cannot stand without taking transaction finality into account. A consensus mechanism can allow a verified transaction to be added to a blockchain DLT, but a level of confidence is needed to ensure the transaction can't be subsequently revoked, reversed, or changed. For example, if an attacker is able to gain majority control over a blockchain network, referred to as a 51% attack, then the finality of network transactions will be compromised. The attacker could invalidate certain transactions via a fork, or write incorrect information to the ledger. Therefore, we must consider both consensus and transaction finality when reviewing blockchain frameworks for enterprise use cases.

By the end of this chapter, you will have an understanding of how distributed system concepts apply to blockchain, and the origin of today's popular blockchain consensus algorithms such as RAFT, Proof of Work, and Proof of Stake.

Properties of Distributed Systems

In general, a distributed system includes nodes or actors working together over a network to perform tasks. Add the notion of decentralization, and you have a system in which work is performed with no central authority governing the actions or outcomes. Nodes exchange messages to communicate with one another, and this activity needs to be secure and synchronized in an environment not guaranteed to be 100 percent reliable.

Distributed systems have several properties and concerns. Nodes operate simultaneously and independently, failure can occur at various levels in the architecture, communication is needed between potentially thousands of geographically dispersed nodes, and it is difficult to have one global or central coordinator to keep all participants in sync. Not an easy set of considerations to address. To start, we'll begin by describing two primary concepts related to blockchain and consensus: the means of communication used to support message passing, and the ability of the network to handle different types of faults. These concepts, when combined with the properties of consensus mentioned previously, serve as great background to the various consensus algorithms proposed or in use today.

Message Passing and Communication Patterns

To transfer messages or data over a distributed network, several communication patterns may be used, including synchronous, partially synchronous, or asynchronous. With synchronous message passing, strong guarantees are provided about the behavior of the distributed system. Messages are delivered without arbitrary delays and within a known upper time bound, and message delivery is typically ordered between nodes via synchronized clocks. Synchronous message passing makes it easier to achieve consensus because nodes can operate according to known time limits and guarantees and be assured data is delivered.

However, in the real world, this pattern has issues. It is impractical to assume delays will not occur across a network, and global message ordering across a distributed system is very difficult to achieve due to issues such as clock drift. Therefore, while synchronous message passing may be found in a small permissioned blockchain network located within a data center where you have control over the network and the infrastructure, it is not feasible for large permissioned deployments or permissionless networks.

In comparison, asynchronous message passing does not make any assumptions about the delivery time of messages or their order. Messages may be delivered at any point in time or dropped altogether, and clock synchronization or local clock timestamps are not involved in determining message order. This greatly improves the scalability of the system and makes the network more resilient to faults, but does increase its complexity. Nodes cannot use known timeouts to detect faults, there is no delay guarantee, and duplication or non-delivery of messages can occur.

With asynchronous message passing, research has also shown that consensus cannot be guaranteed, even in the event of a single faulty process or crash failure. Referred to as the "FLP impossibility,"[23] the result of needing to accommodate for node failure at any time and in the presence of unbounded delivery guarantees, is the possibility of a window of time in which the entire algorithm will wait indefinitely to reach termination. Given the need to satisfy various consensus conditions, the unpredictable behavior of this form of message passing makes achieving consensus difficult.

Finally, partially synchronous message passing includes aspects of the synchronous and asynchronous options. Message delivery is

---

[23] Michael Fisher, Nancy Lynch, and Michael Paterson, "Impossibility of Distributed Consensus with One Faulty Process," *Journal of the Association for Computing Machinery* 32, no. 2 (April 1985): 374–82, https://groups.csail.mit.edu/tds/papers/Lynch/jacm85.pdf.

guaranteed, but the requirement of a fixed and well-defined time boundary is relaxed somewhat to accommodate delays.

For blockchain networks, it has historically been more practical to base consensus on partially synchronous or asynchronous messaging. However, given the FLP impossibility problem, complete asynchronous behavior does require a certain amount of "rule bending" for consensus to be reached, something I describe later in this chapter.

Crash and Byzantine Fault Tolerance

As previously mentioned, building distributed systems is hard. Challenges include data synchronization, transaction ordering and performance, issues with peer-to-peer networks and node reliability, and the class of attacks to which these systems are exposed. Components of the system may crash, data may not be received by one or more nodes, and in some cases, random or malicious behavior by certain nodes in the network must be detected and prevented. This last challenge is especially important for blockchain networks supporting exchanges of value; nodes that deviate from the core protocol can quickly destroy the system, even if it is resilient to system crashes.

Subsequently, any successful approach to building reliable distributed systems needs to consider two factors: crash fault tolerance and Byzantine Fault Tolerance.

Crash fault tolerance allows the system to work regardless of failures in its components. If a node crashes—a segment of the network loses connectivity, or data is unable to be delivered—the entire system should not halt. However, a crash fault-tolerant system does not necessarily handle Byzantine or malicious behavior. If a node attempts to perform operations outside of the best interests of the network, a crash fault-tolerant system will not provide protection. In this case, a Byzantine fault tolerant system is needed.

Byzantine faults are derived from the Byzantine Generals Problem outlined in the oft-cited research paper, "The Byzantine Generals Problem," released by Leslie Lamport, Robert Shostak, and Marshall Pease in 1982. This paper presents a military analogy to a long-standing computer science problem: how to deal with consensus in distributed, and sometimes untrustworthy, peer-to-peer networked systems. The research shows that for normal processing to occur in such a system, the system must have at least $3f + 1$ total nodes, where f is the number of Byzantine nodes. At this point, the number of malicious or faulty nodes will be outnumbered by properly behaving nodes, and consensus can be achieved.

With blockchain, the need for crash fault tolerance is obvious, and some form of this capability will exist in most common blockchain networks. For Byzantine Fault Tolerance, however, the need depends on network type. In a permissioned network, the requirement to handle Byzantine faults is often minimal, because participants are known, and the likelihood of malicious actors being allowed to participate in the network or gain control over a node is low. However, in an open or permissionless network, this requirement increases, and a more secure, comprehensive approach is needed. A number of approaches for both crash and Byzantine Fault Tolerance are described later in this chapter, but be aware that blockchain capabilities in this area vary greatly. When comparing technologies, it is important to understand how these features are supported along with any related trade-offs.

Replicated State

The last aspect of general distributed systems I cover in this chapter is state management, the ability for nodes to eventually derive a consistent and agreed-upon copy of data in response to client requests. The problem of state in distributed systems is not new, and much research has been done in this area. For our purposes, I will start by comparing blockchain's core processing characteristics to those of another common computer science concept, the replicated state machine.

Used to describe various types of software systems, including anything from compilers to event-driven systems, replicated state machine processing is relatively straightforward. The system starts in an initial state and responds to events received from outside actors. As events arrive, each event is evaluated against a rule or state transition function, which determines if the state machine should transition or move to a new state. This process repeats, with the system using consensus to ensure all nodes agree and terminate on these new values. The cycle continues, and as this happens, if all nodes in a distributed network maintain a copy of this state, the state machine is said to be replicated.

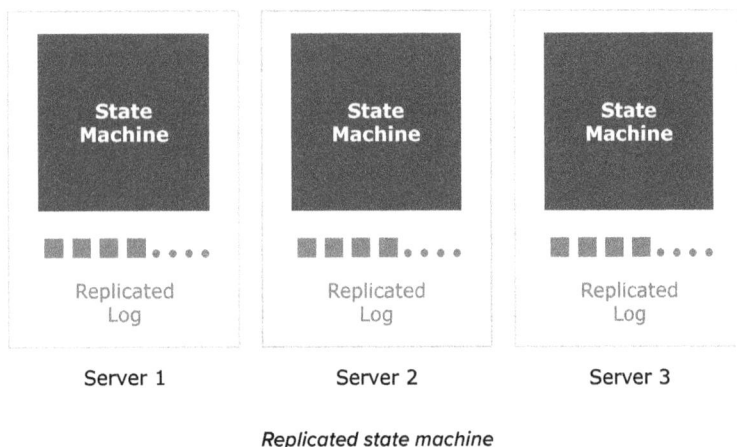

Replicated state machine

This should sound familiar because blockchain has a very similar approach to handling transactions. First, when a blockchain is formed, an initial state called the genesis block is instantiated. As blocks are created from transactions and added to the blockchain DLT according to the rules of the network, a state change is triggered. This state change is then replicated across the peer-to-peer network to participating nodes. Each node applies the network's rules against the data, and if agreement is reached on the final outcome, the node adds the data to its copy of the ledger. If all nodes required to reach agreement do so, then consensus is achieved, and each node has the same view of system state. This achieves the goals of the network and ensures participants have a consistent, agreed-upon view of all transactions.

At this point, you have enough background to tackle the next section of this chapter: specific techniques designed to address the problem of consensus. As I describe these, also remember that node behavior is not necessarily consistent. Nodes can start as non-faulty, but shift to faulty at any time. Faults can be caused by a crash or other technical issue, but can also be due to less obvious factors such as a change to the network's incentive system. This change is especially possible in permissionless blockchain networks because there is typically no consortium or over-arching governing body. If it is more profitable or desirable for a node to behave differently, then it is likely that a certain number of nodes will deviate from the expected protocol and become Byzantine.

TYPES OF CONSENSUS MECHANISMS

When looking at different types of consensus techniques, it's first important to note that, although it would be optimal to combine a Byzantine fault tolerant system with a completely asynchronous environment, research has shown this to be improbable without relaxing certain constraints. This is especially true if deterministic or absolute transaction finality is expected, where each new computed state is deemed to be final, either instantly or after a certain number of steps. As a result, with distributed systems and blockchain, achieving consensus typically requires shifting to synchronous or partially synchronous message passing, or using probabilistic instead of deterministic consensus.

Second, you have likely heard about mining in blockchain. Consensus algorithms are related to the concept of mining, which provides additional mechanisms to protect against "Sybil" attacks, situations where attackers attempt to gain majority control of the network through the creation of "fake" nodes under their control. With mining, a dynamically adjusted cost is introduced for nodes to participate in a network, making it very costly and impractical for malicious actors to successfully execute such an attack. Bitcoin is a great example of the use of mining within its Proof of Work consensus model; the level of compute power needed to gain control over the network is a huge barrier to anyone wishing to carry out a Sybil attack. Mining is not included in every consensus approach, but some popular permissionless systems include this capability as an additional way of securing transactions.

Paxos

Paxos (https://en.wikipedia.org/wiki/Paxos_(computer_science)) is a replicated state machine consensus algorithm, and one of the first to be widely adopted as a way to solve the problem of consensus in distributed systems. It relaxes the strict guidelines of asynchronous message passing, and is typically implemented as a partially synchronous system with timeouts to achieve termination and agreement. It solves the problem of crash fault tolerance, but does not address Byzantine Fault Tolerance. This, along with many open or ill-defined implementation details, makes Paxos complex to understand and implement, and so rarely found in blockchain networks.

Raft

Raft (https://raft.github.io/) is another replicated state machine consensus algorithm introduced as an alternative to Paxos. Designed to be more understandable than Paxos, Raft also uses a partially synchronous approach with timeouts to reach consensus across a distributed system. It provides crash fault tolerance, is available as open source with a number of implementations, and is provided as a configurable option in blockchain frameworks such as Hyperledger Fabric and R3 Corda.

Byzantine Fault Tolerance (BFT)

Byzantine fault tolerant consensus algorithms, as discussed earlier, are designed to solve "The Byzantine Generals Problem." Nodes may act maliciously, or be driven by economic incentives to act outside of the intended network protocol. Given the role many blockchains play in recording and transferring value, it's necessary to add Byzantine fault tolerant capabilities to the network to ensure any written transactions are secure, agreed upon, and correct.

Various BFT algorithms have been defined, but one early example receiving widespread recognition is the "Practical Byzantine Fault

Tolerance" (PBFT) algorithm by Castro and Liskov (1999).[24] Designed to improve on the performance of earlier BFT approaches, PBFT builds on the replicated state machine concept and is able to tolerate Byzantine faults. A leader model is used, where a selected leader is responsible for sending client requests to participating nodes, collecting replies, and determining if agreement was reached on the result. The leader may be changed under various conditions, and if the proposed transaction is agreed upon by the nodes, then it is deemed to be final.

PBFT introduced a real-world approach to addressing Byzantine faults. However, in non-optimized form, PBFT requires a substantial amount of communication between nodes and is also susceptible to Sybil attacks. This makes it impractical for blockchain deployments outside of smaller permissioned networks. Other protocols, however, have since been introduced to solve some of these shortcomings, with platforms such as Hyperledger Sawtooth and Tendermint including consensus approaches derived from BFT or PBFT concepts.

Proof of Work (PoW)

No surprise here! Proof of Work is likely one of the best-known, discussed, and debated consensus algorithms in use today. A quick search on the internet will yield a substantial amount of information

---

[24] Miguel Castro and Barbara Liskov, "Practical Byzantine Fault Tolerance" in *Proceedings of the Third Symposium on Operating Systems Design and Implementation* (New Orleans, February 1999), http://pmg.csail.mit.edu/papers/osdi99.pdf.

on it, which I won't try to include in this chapter. However, PoW is a key breakthrough in the world of blockchain consensus, and a book on blockchain would not be complete without a discussion of it.

Made popular in 2009 when Bitcoin became the first blockchain network to incorporate Proof of Work ("Nakamoto") as its consensus algorithm, it may surprise you to learn that Proof of Work was actually created a number of years prior. Originally designed to deter spammers,[25] PoW requires a node to expend computational effort to calculate a specific output or value before a process or task (such as sending an email) can be executed. Once calculated, this value can be easily transmitted and verified by other nodes in the network and serves as proof that a certain amount of work was performed as a prerequisite to the task. This work has a cost, and by requiring nodes to incur this cost, a PoW system discourages bad actors because their malicious actions (sending *lots* of emails) are not financially possible or profitable.

With blockchains such as Bitcoin, Proof of Work is used in a similar fashion, with a few key additions:

First, communication is achieved via a gossip protocol over the peer-to-peer network, where nodes are only connected to a subset of (not all) nodes, and messages are sent among that subset ("gossiped").

---

[25] One example: Wikipedia, s.v. "Hashcash," last modified May 2, 2022, 23:21 (UTC), https://en.wikipedia.org/wiki/Hashcash.

Second, the concept of mining is introduced, where a number of nodes, called miners, participate in a computationally expensive "guessing game" before any blocks are added to the blockchain DLT. To win this game, a miner attempts to be the first to calculate a special value called a nonce, include this value in a block, and send this block to the network. The nonce may only be derived via trial-and-error, and the complexity of finding this value is automatically adjusted by the network. If the value becomes too easy to find, then the network makes the game harder. After verification of the value is complete, the block is added to the ledger, the winning node is rewarded, and the competition continues with the next block. This happens across the network, which in the case of Bitcoin, is a substantial number of miners.

This process results in an interesting outcome. With a large network such as Bitcoin, the need to prove a certain amount of work before a block is written makes it very difficult for a bad actor to impact overall network security. A substantial amount of expensive compute power would be needed to take control, and the characteristics of the underlying blockchain data structure result in the need for bad actors to build blocks faster than all other nodes, something that is extremely difficult to achieve.

Third, Proof of Work blockchains shift to probabilistic rather than deterministic consensus. Rather than requiring each node to communicate to every other node via synchronous interactions to reach agreement and termination, PoW uses a "longest chain" approach as a way to reach consensus in an asynchronous manner. As miners add blocks to the underlying DLT, it is possible to temporarily have more than one chain. Two miners, for example, can simultaneously solve the nonce puzzle and add their block to the ledger, leading to a "fork." At this point, other miners may choose to continue with either chain, and the mining process continues.

However, over time, one chain will start to outgrow the other and become the main chain, leaving the other chain's transactions orphaned. Until this fork is resolved, or until the possibility of a fork is minimal, there is a higher probability that a transaction may be rejected. Conversely, as the mining process continues, a state will be reached where it is fairly certain that this exception will no longer occur. This allows the network to diverge for a period of time, either due to a fork or other network issue, but eventually the network will converge and reach agreement on the main chain. The consensus process is probabilistic, because it isn't 100 percent certain that a transaction will not be rejected, but over time, the chances of this occurring shrink.

With Bitcoin, for example, it is recommended to wait for approximately six blocks to be added to the network before a transaction is considered final. Since each block currently takes about 10 minutes to add, which is a rate controlled by the network, a wait time of one hour is expected.

Today, Proof of Work on Bitcoin is one of the few blockchain consensus implementations that has proven to be successful, both in terms of adoption and in its ability to secure the network. Another popular network, Ethereum, also currently uses Proof of Work, although this is changing as will be noted in the next section. However, Proof of Work does have a few issues that impact both permissioned and permissionless networks.

First, the need to perform work via mining, often done via specialized hardware such as application-specific integrated circuits (ASICs), makes the algorithm resource-intensive. This is not an issue for small deployments, but it does raise concerns about the environmental impact of large-scale deployments such as Bitcoin.

Second, PoW blockchains often suffer from performance issues and are not designed to handle the latency or throughput of transactions required in many enterprise use cases.

Finally, a large network of nodes is needed to properly secure the network because it would be relatively easy for a bad actor to gain control over a small network with a limited number of transactions or blocks in the DLT. As a result, it is rare to find an enterprise or permissioned blockchain deployment based on PoW; better options are available.

Proof of Stake (PoS)

As with Proof of Work, the Proof of Stake consensus algorithm was made popular by the permissionless Ethereum blockchain network—not because Ethereum uses Proof of Stake (it uses Proof of Work at the time of this writing), but because it is transitioning to Proof of Stake. The move is being watched by many because, if successful, it could solve many of the issues with Proof of Work, including transaction scalability and environmental sustainability.

With Proof of Stake, the need to use specialized hardware to perform expensive computations is removed. Instead of using a competitive mining process, block validators in PoS are selected based on their amount of economic stake, and in some cases the amount of time in which they have held that stake in the network. The validator selection process is deterministic because the probability of being selected to generate a block is proportional to the stake a validator possesses. This makes the block validation process more resource-efficient than Proof of Work, and also offers additional opportunities to increase the overall performance of the network while maintaining security.

However, since expensive compute resources are not required, the incentives for preventing malicious attacks are different from PoW. With Proof of Stake, the validators are typically compensated in the form of a built-in inflation structure and transaction fees, while malicious attacks are deterred by the threat of penalties, including losing one's stake in the network and possibly participation in it. Some argue, however, that these penalties are not strong enough to deter attackers. If a fork occurs in the main chain, for example, a basic implementation of PoS will not disincentivize a validator from attempting to validate against both chains because there is no penalty for doing so. This increases the validator's chances of selecting the winning fork and collecting the transaction fees, but at a cost to the overall behavior and accuracy of the system. This issue is not present with PoW because the compute required to validate against a single chain is substantial, and it is not feasible to split this capability across multiple chains. With PoS, however, unless some form of penalty is built into the system, this "nothing at stake" attack represents a risk to the network.

Many variations of the Proof of Stake consensus algorithm are on the market, from chain-based PoS implementations that mimic PoW functionality with simulated mining, to approaches that combine PoS concepts with BFT. Tendermint, Cardano, and Ethereum's approach to PoS are examples of blockchain frameworks based on Proof of Stake variations. Transaction finality also varies with these implementations, with methods ranging from immediate to probabilistic finality, plus the inclusion of economic finality where exceedingly expensive penalties are incurred if a bad actor attempts to maliciously influence the finality of a transaction. Given the interest and research in this area, it is likely that these offerings will continue to evolve to support the needs of enterprise use cases.

Other Options

At this point, I have only touched on a handful of blockchain consensus algorithms. As mentioned, these algorithms are seen as a differentiating feature for blockchain platforms, and are constantly evolving. Dozens of variations exist, with a few listed in the following table.

Proof of Work	Proof of Capacity / Space
Proof of Stake	SPECTRE - Serialized PoW
Delegated Proof of Stake	Proof of Stake Velocity
Proof of Elapsed time	Delayed Proof of Work
Proof of History	Proof of Importance
Proof of Space Time	Proof of Bandwidth
Proof of Stake Time	Proof of Ownership
Practical Proof of Kernel Work	Proof of Intelligence
Proof of Authority	Proof of Burn
Proof of Contribution	Ouroboros (PoS variant)
Proof of Retrievability	Proof of Time
Proof of Use	Proof of Asset
Proof of Access	Proof of Activity
Proof of Reputable Observation	Resulted Delegated Proof of Stake
Proof of CAPTCHA	Adaptive Proof of Work
Proof of Resource	Leased Proof of Stake
Proof of Believability	Dynamic Proof of Stake
Proof of Coverage	Proof of Process
Proof of Weight	Proof of Participation
Proof of Reputation	Proof of Involvement & Integrity
Proof of Existence	Proof of Influence

Sample consensus systems used/proposed in the market

Each algorithm attempts to address the problems of agreement, termination, crash fault tolerance, and Byzantine Fault Tolerance in a decentralized, distributed network of honest or malicious participants. The success of a blockchain network is dependent on consensus, making understanding differences between each algorithm extremely important, including:

- Compute resources required

- Level of transaction finality

- Time to reach transaction finality

- Associated incentive system

- Performance

- Ability to handle Byzantine behavior and crash fault tolerance

- Message passing and underlying communications protocol

Additionally, organizations are now looking at consensus "as a service," where the consensus algorithm becomes a pluggable component of a blockchain framework. This offers the opportunity to switch from one algorithm to another without changing the entire framework, to reduce vendor lock-in, and enable the creation of application-specific blockchains with consensus algorithms optimized for a specific use case.

GOVERNING WITH CONSENSUS

Consensus may be used to not only reach agreement on transactions, but also on network governance rules. In the permissionless world, governance consensus was first attempted in 2016 through the creation of the DAO, or the Decentralized Autonomous Organization, on the Ethereum network. The goal was to introduce an entity completely automated through code in the blockchain and remove any need for a centralized governing authority. Unfortunately, this structure failed due to security vulnerabilities and code errors, but the basic concept of using consensus, along with constructs such as smart contracts, to create any form of a DAO is still feasible.

For example, in a permissioned network, consensus may be reached to determine how the network will operate via voting. Who is allowed to join the network? How will network changes be handled? How will errors be acknowledged or handled? The logic behind these questions may be built into the network via smart contracts, with known or specifically identified participants having a vote on the outcome. In the ideal case, the result is a network in which no central authority controls the decisions, and an agreed-upon consensus process is used to automate actions that manage the network. Realistically, however, this specific use of consensus in a permissioned or enterprise context is likely to be combined with traditional legal agreements and other regulatory considerations. Until it is possible to capture the nuances and complexities of governance in code, the use of a hybrid governance model is needed.

FINAL THOUGHTS

By now it should be obvious that consensus is a very complex topic! Different message passing patterns, the need to securely satisfy various conditions within the constraints of distributed networks, support for crash or Byzantine Fault Tolerance, a multitude of state replication strategies, and transaction finality and settlement make consensus a much-researched, often-debated subject. If you decide to dig deeper, be prepared to enjoy many hours of research!

Before moving on, I want to make one more comment on consensus and its impact. Many enterprises, wanting to preserve their reputation and not be seen as wasteful to their customers, are hesitant to be associated with resource-intensive consensus algorithms such as Proof of Work. Investors are also increasingly looking at non-financial factors as part of their analysis processes, and any organization seen to be contradicting popular environmental, social, or governance (ESG) factors runs the risk of receiving negative press and attention. Will this impact Bitcoin or cause companies to use other networks? Only time will tell.

Now, let's shift gears, take a break from technology, and look at the problem of identity.

Chapter 8

THE NEW IDENTITY

*The internet was built without a way to know who and what
you are connecting to. This limits what we can do with it and
exposes us to growing dangers. If we do nothing, we will face
rapidly proliferating episodes of theft and deception which
will cumulatively erode public trust in the internet.*

—Kim Cameron, "The Laws of Identity"[26]

Identity-related challenges have plagued us for a long time. The ability to prove who you are is critical to dozens of tasks: banking, driving, purchasing goods and services, logging into applications and
websites, even going to the gym. Establishing identity requires trust,
safety, privacy, and security between people and organizations,
often without direct knowledge of all the parties involved. Identity
is complex, but necessary, and hundreds of books and articles have
been written about it. Covering just one aspect of identity can take

---

[26] Kim Cameron, "The Laws of Identity," Kim Cameron's Identity Weblog (blog), May
2005, https://www.identityblog.com/stories/2005/05/13/TheLawsOfIdentity.pdf.

hundreds of pages! However, given its importance and relevance to blockchain, and today's accelerated need to streamline associated processes, I'm including a discussion on identity in this book.

As Cameron wrote in "The Laws of Identity," the internet was not designed with identity in mind. However, if the internet is to continue to be the means by which people and organizations interact, then an identity system that is secure, private, consistent, reliable, and easy to use is necessary. It should be open, accessible by all, and transparent, with appropriate levels of standardization and collaboration across organizations and regulatory bodies. If all this can be achieved, it is possible our lives will be greatly simplified, and we'll enjoy even better trust, privacy, and security.

However, before we reach this state of nirvana, plenty of work needs to be done. In this chapter, I focus on the emerging concepts, standards, and effects of identity and describe how approaches such as decentralized identity (DID) and self-sovereign identity (SSI) are shifting the balance of power from large enterprises back to the individual. And while blockchain is not a mandatory component of these methods, it offers advantages, which I also cover.

MOVING IDENTITY TO THE DIGITAL WORLD

Many readers will have heard of the country of Estonia, and its support for digital identifiers in many government and enterprise functions. Since 1997, citizens of Estonia have been performing common tasks digitally, such as voting, establishing a company, banking, document signing and transmitting, making healthcare appointments, and numerous other e-services.

"Every Estonian, irrespective of their location, has a state issued digital identity, and every person can provide digital signatures through a number of solutions so they can safely identify themselves and use e-services."[27] Estonia has even built and deployed its own version of blockchain, the KSI Blockchain, after experiencing a series of cyberattacks in 2007. With KSI Blockchain, "Systems and data are free of compromise, all while retaining 100% data privacy."[28]

For Estonians, digital identity is a way of life. But for many other countries, alternative views on privacy, security, and trust in government have slowed the creation and deployment of digital identity solutions. However, with today's accelerated digital transformation initiatives, a shift in consumer behavior towards online interactions, and increased focus on security and privacy, the importance of digital identity and better identity systems is becoming critical.

---

[27] "e-Identity," e-Estonia website, https://e-estonia.com/solutions/e-identity/id-card/.

[28] "Cyber Security," e-Estonia website, https://e-estonia.com/solutions/cyber-security/ksi-blockchain/.

What Is Digital Identity?

Kim Cameron defined digital identity as "a set of claims made by one digital subject about itself or another digital subject."[29] Digital subjects may be people, organizations, devices, relationships, or other nonhuman elements; claims express attributes or facts about the subjects, such as "age > 21."

To describe it a different way, think of digital identities as verified, electronic representations of subjects used to prove certain characteristics or facts. Identities can be used for authentication, authorization, or in transactions to ensure all subjects can trust each other. Furthermore, identities are not just about common attributes, such as name, address, social security number, and birthdate. They can also include information on preferences, personal interests, past behaviors, or even relationships, all elements describing who we are.

The ways identity is managed today, however, are fraught with issues. Current identity models are limited, with control removed from digital subjects. Before getting into decentralized or self-sovereign identity, it is important to review today's identity models, starting with those involving people and later addressing organizations and devices.

[29] Cameron, "Identity."
https://www.identityblog.com/stories/2005/05/13/TheLawsOfIdentity.pdf.

Current Digital Identity Models

How many usernames and passwords do you have for logging into websites? How many logins do you perform through accounts held by third parties such as Google or Facebook?

These questions reveal two of today's most common identity models. The first is direct identity where username/password combinations, personal identification numbers (PINs), biometrics, or other methods directly authenticate and convey your identity to a third party. Verification questions, two-factor authentication, or hardware or software tokens are often used to strengthen security. These credentials and other "secrets," such as answers to personal questions, are stored by the third party, and separate relationships are created for each distinct interaction. Banking websites, retail sites, and many others follow this model, making it the most popular way to identify individuals.

The second model is referred to as the federated or provider identity (IDP) model. In this implementation, an organization or service such as Google, Facebook, or Instagram acts as an identity provider for third-party applications. Users have an account with the IDP, and this account may be used to authenticate to another application through protocols such as OAuth, SAML, or OpenID Connect (OIDC). This federation or forwarding of credentials happens automatically via the IDP, with nothing special required by the user. The user simply logs into the IDP, and the service does the rest. As with the direct identity model, additional mechanisms may be used to increase security, and identity-related data is managed and stored by the IDP.

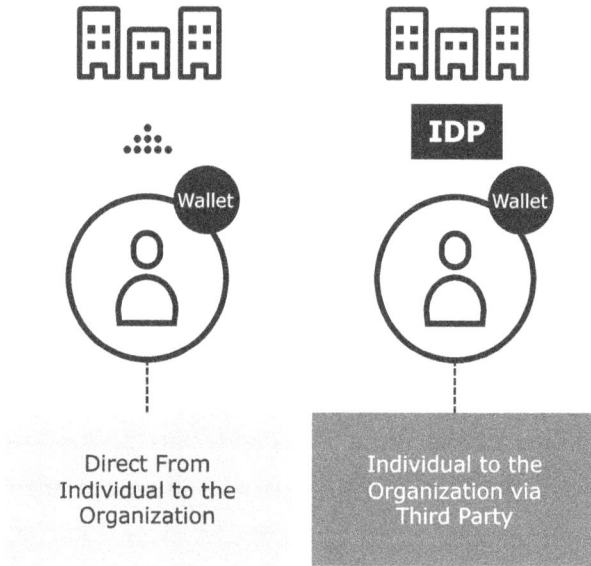

Typical identity relationships

These identity models should be familiar to most readers. The models have been used for years, and entire software solutions have emerged to assist with common problems such as password and token management. However, in today's increasingly digital world, both methods are becoming insufficient due to issues including:

- **Use of insecure passwords.** "123456" or "Password1" are obviously not great choices, but unfortunately, they are some of the most common passwords used today.[30] People simply have too many passwords to remember, and thus resort to passwords that are easy to remember, repeated, or even written on paper. Identity theft, fraud, and data breaches are just a few of the results of improper password selection and management.

- **Loss of control over personal information.** Profile or personal information is stored by organizations outside the control of the individual. What security systems do these organizations (which may include small businesses) use to keep this information secure and private? Can these systems be trusted? There are numerous examples of inadequate technologies or processes being used where loss of identity data resulted.

- **Centralization of control.** Centralization of an IDP introduces various risks. If the IDP becomes unavailable, then all access to associated third-party applications is blocked until the service is reinstated. IDPs can control or suddenly restrict access to their services (again, blocking access to third parties), and if the organization acting as

---

[30] Pete Mitchell, "100 Most Common Passwords of 2022. Can You Spot Your Password?" Tech Cult, January 2, 2022, https://techcult.com/most-common-passwords/.

an IDP fails to make a profit, money spent on security and other safety measures may be reduced, putting personal information at greater risk.

- **Exclusion of the individual from the value chain.** Because of their role, many IDPs have a large amount of personal information. This data has tremendous value, which is not shared with the individuals who provided it. Instead, the IDP is the one that profits, whether through legitimate or questionable[31] means.

- **Limited flexibility and scalability.** While maintaining direct connections with all parties for which they act as identity providers, IDPs dictate the mechanisms and policies used to collect, store, and use the information. Options for individuals to manage their own identity information are limited, as is the scalability or architecture of identity networks.

Overall, the problem is one of control, or rather loss of control by the individual. Instead, separate organizations or a few large IDPs have it all. IDPs force individuals to create relationships separate from the organizations they are targeting. Furthermore, the ability

---

[31] Wikipedia, s.v. "Facebook–Cambridge Analytica data scandal," last modified June 2, 2022, 15:51 (UTC), https://en.wikipedia.org/wiki/Facebook%E2%80%93Cambridge_Analytica_data_scandal.

for individuals to revoke or change their identity information is limited because of data duplication and loss of visibility, and the entire approach is extremely siloed and centralized. In essence, individuals rent their identity to IDPs, putting their identity out of their control and at risk, especially if an IDP decides to shut down an account or even leave the market.

What if digital identity could be put back into the hands of the individual? How would it work, and where does blockchain fit? To answer these questions, we need to look at new technologies gaining traction in the industry, including decentralized and self-sovereign identity.

GIVING IDENTITY BACK TO THE INDIVIDUAL

Technical identity systems must only reveal information identifying a user with the user's consent...the system must be designed to put the user in control of what digital identities are used, and what information is released.[32]

Kim Cameron's first Law of Identity places the focus back on the individual, which is also the underlying principle of self-sovereign identity (SSI). With SSI, users maintain control over their identity,

---

[32] Cameron, "Identity,"
https://www.identityblog.com/stories/2005/05/13/TheLawsOfIdentity.pdf.

verify their identity information is going to a trusted target, and determine what information to share. An individual's identity information is not stored or held by third parties or centralized organizations and, when combined with cryptography techniques such as zero-knowledge proofs, certain claims can be provided as proof without revealing the details behind those claims. SSI moves identity towards becoming decentralized, streamlined, standardized, and flexible, with improved security and privacy. There are issues and barriers to overcome as I will soon describe, but the limitations of current identity models make alternative approaches such as SSI a key success factor in the digitalization of future enterprise products and services.

One quick note before I continue. PKI or public key encryption is a key (no pun intended) component of SSI. Public and private keys are used extensively to verify credentials, prevent tampering, share proofs, establish peer connections, and enable various other functions. I've touched on the topic of PKI in previous chapters, but you may want to quickly refresh your memory before continuing if you are not familiar with this concept.

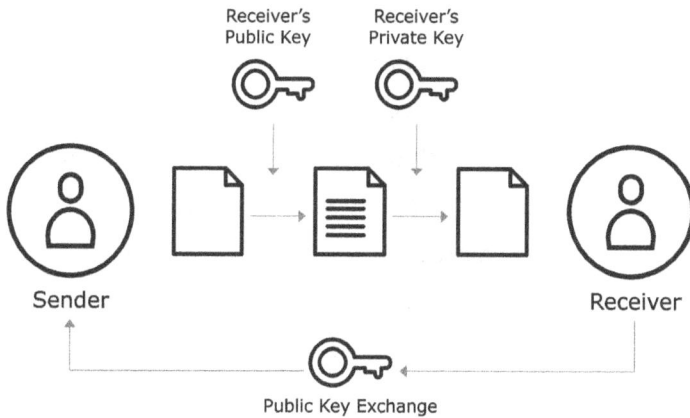

Public key cryptography

Self-Sovereign Identity

The ability for an individual to generate public-private key pairs, securely manage private keys, store and exchange public keys, generate and share proofs, and do so with a streamlined user experience, are important functions of self-sovereign identity systems. To support these needs, SSI typically uses a digital wallet whose function may be thought of as similar to a physical wallet. This digital wallet, provided by an online service, hardware device, or software application installed on something like a mobile device, is used to store identifiers, cryptographic keys, verifiable credentials, and more. For example, a wallet may store common credentials such as a passport, driver's license, or health card, or it may store other useful information such as educational background, employment history, or proof of skills such as a pilot's license.

Individuals use this wallet to securely interact with the underlying SSI system while maintaining control over shared information. A wallet streamlines the functions needed to make SSI work, and provides a secure place to store personal information. However, just like a physical wallet, you do not want to lose your digital wallet! There are strategies for recovering the contents of a digital wallet should the device or account be stolen or access lost, but as many Bitcoin private wallet holders have discovered, regaining access is not always possible.

Beyond wallets, SSI comprises many other foundational components, many of which are explained in the remainder of this chapter. I align the discussion with the work currently being performed by the W3C, Decentralized Identity Foundation (https://identity.foundation/), and the Linux Foundation (https://trustoverip.org/). As mentioned, there are many variations of digital identity and SSI in the market. Common specifications and methods are emerging, with many being driven by these three organizations along with industry partners such as Microsoft, IBM, and Evernym (https://www.evernym.com/). Standards convergence is important to the success of SSI solutions because it will simplify platform interoperability and drive broader adoption.

Foundational Elements of Self-Sovereign Identity

Trust Triangle

SSI involves the exchange of credentials between three core roles: issuers, holders, and verifiers. Issuers, including individuals and organizations like banks or government agencies, are responsible for creating credentials. Holders are the recipients of credentials. They respond to verifiers' requests for credentials (or portions of credentials) and use wallets for credential management. Verifiers consist of any party wishing to verify that credentials or claims made by a holder are accurate and trusted. Together, these roles form a "trust triangle"[33] representing the interactions that occur in a self-sovereign identity system.

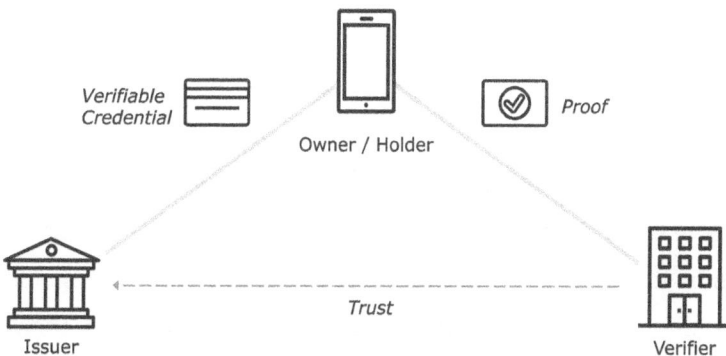

Verifiable Credential

Owner / Holder

Proof

Issuer

Trust

Verifier

Three core roles of SSI

---

[33] Wikipedia, s.v. "Self-sovereign identity," last modified March 2, 2022, 16:26, https://en.wikipedia.org/wiki/Self-sovereign_identity.

There are variations of this trust triangle. It's possible, for example, for holders to establish private connections directly to other holders to exchange credentials over a mutually established and secure channel. Certain responsibilities may be delegated by the holder to another party to allow them to perform certain functions on the holder's behalf; for example, a guardianship agreement might be arranged for people who cannot directly manage or access their digital credentials. In most cases, the trust triangle and its roles exist in SSI exchanges.

Verifiable Credentials

Credentials are tricky to define because there is no one type or form. They may be issued by governments, corporations, and other institutions, or be self-asserted and generated by the holder. Credentials consist of one or more claims (attributes) applied against a particular subject (for example, a person, organization, or device), and can not only be issued, but also revoked by an issuer. However, regardless of their type or how they are generated, it is important that issued credentials are considered accurate and true by holders and verifiers, or the entire system falls apart. With SSI, this state is achieved through the use of key pairs, key registration, trust registries, public utilities, and other components that I cover in the following sections.

No form of cryptography can address the problem of how to verify issuers in the first place, and ensure they do not act maliciously within the system. Some issuers are usually more trustworthy, such as governments or educational institutions, or in many cases the value of the credential does not require a high degree of trust (such as a retail loyalty points card). Other situations, however, require formal governing structures such as an overarching consortium. These structures act as underlying trust anchors[34] and are responsible for ensuring the overall integrity of the participants in the identity system.

Credentials are not only difficult to define, but their many different forms make it challenging to securely exchange, verify, and digitally represent them. To address these issues, the W3C has created the Verifiable Credentials Data Model, which provides a "standard way to express credentials on the Web in a way that is cryptographically secure, privacy respecting, and machine-verifiable."[35]

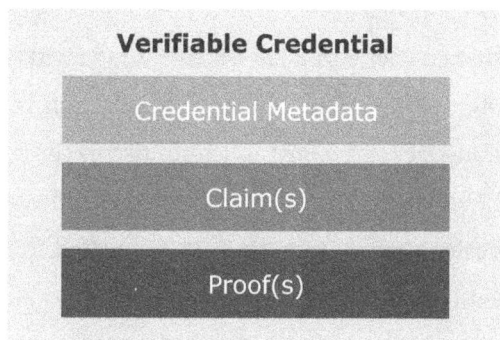

Verifiable Credential

Credential Metadata

Claim(s)

Proof(s)

Components of a verifiable credential

---

[34] Wikipedia, s.v. "Trust anchor," last modified March 30, 2022, 18:33, https://en.wikipedia.org/wiki/Trust_anchor.

[35] *Verifiable Credentials Data Model v1.1 (W3C Recommendation)*, (W3C, March 3, 2022), https://www.w3.org/TR/vc-data-model/.

Issuers, holders, and verifiers use this standardized model when exchanging, storing, and retrieving credentials and identity information across the trust triangle, improving interoperability, and reducing dependencies on a particular technology.

Decentralized Identifiers, Methods, and Communication

With PKI, wallets, and verifiable credentials as building blocks, I now turn to the systems that coordinate and manage the flow of information across the trust triangle. Again, the W3C and Decentralized Identity Foundation (DIF) provide the starting point, with the industry creating specifications to assist with the exchange of verified credentials. They include:

- **DID:** "Decentralized identifiers (DIDs) are a new type of identifier that enables verifiable, decentralized digital identity. A DID refers to any subject (person, organization, thing, data model, abstract entity, etc.) as determined by the controller of the DID. In contrast to typical, federated identifiers, DIDs have been designed so that they may be decoupled from centralized registries, identity providers, and certificate authorities."[36]

- **DID document:** "A set of data describing the DID subject, including mechanisms, such as cryptographic public keys,

---

[36] *Decentralized Identifiers (DIDs) v1.0: Core Architecture, Data Model, and Representations (W3C Proposed Recommendation),* (W3C, August 3, 2021), https://www.w3.org/TR/did-core/.

that the DID subject or a DID delegate can use to authenticate itself and prove its association with the DID."[37]

- **DID method:** "A DID method defines how implementers
  can realize the features described by this specification. DID
  methods are often associated with a particular verifiable
  data registry. New DID methods are defined in their own
  specifications to enable interoperability between different
  implementations of the same DID method."[38]

- **DIDComm:** "The purpose of DIDComm is to provide a
  secure, private communication methodology built atop the
  decentralized design of DIDs."[39]

By combining these specifications with the aforementioned building blocks, a technical picture of SSI starts to emerge. The diagram
below helps illustrate the role of each component with examples
—issuer (employer), holder (employee), and verifier (bank)—in
an end-to-end identity verification scenario that could take the
following steps:

---

[37] "Section 2: Terminology: DID document," *Decentralized Identifiers (DIDs) v1.0, Core Architecture, Data Model, and Representations (W3C Proposed Recommendation)*, (W3C, August 3, 2021), https://www.w3.org/TR/did-core/#dfn-did-documents.

[38] "Section 8: Methods," *Decentralized Identifiers (DIDs) v1.0: Core Architecture, Data Model, and Representations (W3C Proposed Recommendation)*, (W3C, August 3, 2021), https://www.w3.org/TR/did-core/#methods.

[39] Sam Curren, Tobias Looker, and Oliver Terbu, eds. *DIDComm Messaging*, DIF, https://identity.foundation/didcomm-messaging/spec/.

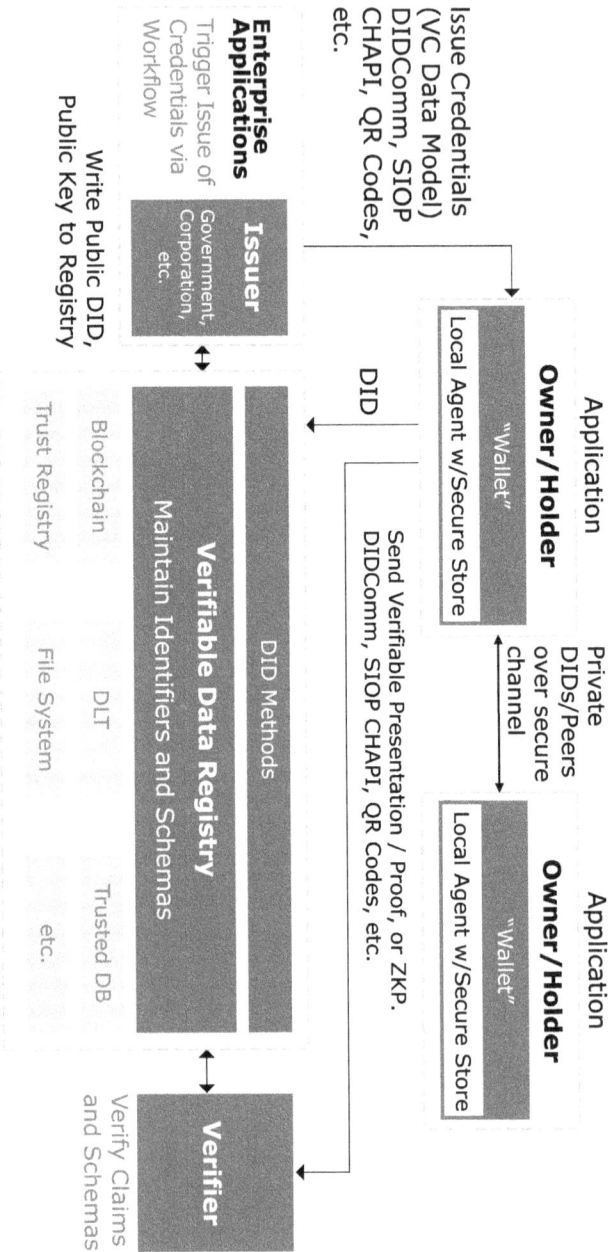

1. The issuer starts by creating a DID, a globally unique persistent identifier that includes a scheme ("did"), corresponding DID method, and a DID method-specific identifier.

Simple DID example (https://www.w3.org/TR/did-core/)

The DID can be thought of as the key in a key-value pair that will be used in later steps to facilitate retrieving information stored as DID documents. The DID method specifies how required DID operations will be realized by the verifiable data registry. For example, provisional DID methods are currently defined for Bitcoin (did:btcr), Corda (did:corda), Sovrin (did:sov), and many others. When a DID operation (such as a DID document lookup) is requested during the verification process, the DID method allows the operation to be mapped to a specific function call in the underlying technology stack. This mapping separates the DID specification from a registry's implementation, which is important because the registry may be based on a variety of technologies including blockchain, DLTs, decentralized file systems, and trusted databases.

2. The DID is bundled into a DID document, along with information about the DID subject. The document can also include authentication details such as the public key corresponding to the private key used by the issuer to sign verifiable credentials.

```
{
  "@context": [
    "https://www.w3.org/ns/did/v1",
    "https://w3id.org/security/suites/ed25519-2020/v1"
  ]
  "id": "did:example:123456789abcdefghi",
  "authentication": [{
    // used to authenticate as did:...fghi
    "id": "did:example:123456789abcdefghi#keys-1",
    "type": "Ed25519VerificationKey2020",
    "controller": "did:example:123456789abcdefghi",
    "publicKeyMultibase": "zH3C2AVvLMv6gmMNam3uVAjZpfkcJCwDwnZn6z3wXmqPV"
  }]
}
```

Simple DID document (https://www.w3.org/TR/did-core/
#example-1-a-simple-did-document)

The DID document is signed and written by the issuer to the verifiable data registry along with the public key. Following our example, the employer now has a public DID and public key entry in the verifiable data registry. As we will see, this information will later be accessed by the verifier as part of a credential verification step.

3. The issuer decides on the data to be included in the verifiable credential and the format in which it will be represented. Various formats are possible, such as JSON-LD, JSON-JWT, or JSON-ZKP-CL. Based on these

decisions, a verifiable credential (VC) conforming to the Verifiable Credentials Data Model is created. For example, the VC for employment verification could include the employee's name, employer details, date of employment, job role, and other relevant information.

4. After the credential is prepared by the issuer for the holder, a direct, secure connection is established between these two roles and the VC is transferred to the holder's wallet. Various connection options are available, including DIDComm, SIOP CHAPI, or QR codes. At this point, the employee has a cryptographically secured employment verification credential issued by their trusted employer.

5. Next, let's assume the employee is applying for a loan, and needs to provide verification of employment to a bank as part of the application process. In today's world, this requirement could involve some form of interaction between the bank and the employer. The bank may wish to verify the employer in addition to the employee, or it may want to directly verify the employee's details instead of trusting a simple email or paper form. However, with SSI, direct interaction does not need to occur between the bank (verifier) and employer (issuer).

6. Upon receiving the request from the verifier for the specific credential or proof, the holder can provide their

consent and use their wallet to assemble the VC into a properly formatted response. Again, various formats are possible, including JSON-LD, JSON-JWT, or JSON-ZKP-CL. This response is referred to as a verifiable presentation (VP), and may be sent to the verifier using connection options such as DIDComm, SIOP CHAPI, or QR codes. Note that with zero-knowledge proofs, the holder can respond with only a subset of the source VC's attributes or claims rather than the entire credential. I provide more details on this topic in the next section.

7. At this point, the bank now has the employee's employment verification information delivered as a verifiable presentation (VP). To verify its validity, the bank will use the issuer's DID (contained within the VP) to resolve (query) the issuer's DID Document and public key from the Verifiable Data Registry. Using the retrieved issuer public key, the verifier can then verify the claims and attributes contained in the holder's credential.

8. Verification complete! The bank (verifier) has verified that the employee (holder) has a set of valid employment verification credentials issued by a trusted employer (issuer). The employee retains control over the credentials, issues only the information needed for the bank verification process, and no interaction occurs between the employer and the bank. The information is also cryptographically

verifiable, allowing for a high degree of trust that the data is valid and has not been altered.

As with any emerging technology, the steps above represent one possible (although most common) set of interactions across the trust triangle. Other interaction patterns exist, including another common model worth mentioning at this point, the ability for parties to create private, direct connections to other parties over a channel established via DIDComm.

Defined previously and highlighted in the example, it is important to understand that DIDComm is not just for the exchange of verifiable credentials. It is also a general messaging protocol layer that is transport agnostic and designed to facilitate the creation of secure, DID-based connections over which parties can exchange any type of message.

For example, as indicated in the previous diagram, holders can choose to enhance their wallet functions through associated software agents. These agents, provided via a software platform, support the exchange of private, peer-to-peer DIDComm[40] messages between parties via DIDs. This is one important difference from the example steps provided because in this case, the public and open verifiable data registry is not needed. Instead, the Peer DID specification

[40] Oskar Deventer et al., *Peer DID Method Specification: Blockchain-Independent Decentralized Identifiers,* (W3C Document, October 12, 2021), https://identity.foundation/peer-did-method-spec/index.html.

defines a protocol that peers can use to directly, securely, privately, and asynchronously exchange DIDs and DID Documents. The protocol simplifies the overall architecture, reduces dependencies on an outside source of truth, improves scalability, and increases both privacy and security because only the parties involved are aware of the connection. Because many use cases only require direct interactions, support for a private, peer-to-peer approach is a valuable capability. This support, when combined with public verifiable data registries, enables a hybrid solution to secure a data exchange, whether for the purposes of sharing credentials or as part of a broader application.

Various other concepts were also mentioned throughout the example steps, including SIOP CHAPI and JSON-LD/JWT. These are important interoperability and data formats, but outside the scope of this book. For now, be aware that different verifiable credential formats and communication options exist, with work proceeding to either converge on a common set of options, or improve interoperability when one standard is not possible.

Partial Claims and Zero-Knowledge Proofs (ZKPs)

When exchanging credentials, it is not always necessary or desired to package entire credentials into a verifiable presentation for delivery to a verifier. A holder may want to keep certain attributes private and only provide what is required to minimize the data shared. Additionally, a holder may want to only prove a certain claim, without sharing any of the attributes used to derive it. For example, in some cases, an individual's exact age is important, while in other cases it is only necessary to prove that their age exceeds a certain threshold (age > 21). With today's credentials, such as a driver's license, it is difficult to prove your age without revealing other details, including birthdate and address. With SSI, however, various methods make this possible.

One approach involves the use of selective disclosure, where a holder may select the attributes to be passed to a verifier. Privacy and security improve because entire credentials are not exposed to the third party. A second option is to use predicates, a feature found in platforms such as Sovrin or Hyperledger Indy. Proofs such as greater than or equal to can be used to prove that an attribute (age) meets a certain condition (> 21) without actually revealing the attribute. And finally, cryptographic approaches such as ZKP-CL (Camenisch-Lysyanskaya) and JSON-LD ZKP with BBS+ signatures[41] use zero-knowledge proofs[42] to:

- Combine multiple verifiable credentials from multiple issuers into a single verifiable presentation without revealing verifiable credentials or subject identifiers to the verifier.

---

[41] Tobias Looker and Orie Steel, eds., *BBS+ Signatures 2020: Draft Community Group Report 03 May 2022*, https://w3c-ccg.github.io/ldp-bbs2020/.

[42] "Section 5.8: Zero-Knowledge Proofs," *Verifiable Credentials Data Model v1.1*, (W3C Recommendation, March 3, 2022), https://w3c.github.io/vc-data-model/#zero-knowledge-proofs.

- Selectively disclose the claims in a verifiable credential to a verifier without requiring issuance of multiple atomic verifiable credentials.

- Produce a derived verifiable credential formatted according to the verifier's data schema instead of the issuer's, without needing to involve the issuer after the verifiable credential is issued.

The ability for a holder to selectively disclose information is a key element of a self-sovereign identity system. To realize maximum potential, users must have the ability to control what attributes are shared and only convey the information necessary to complete a credential verification request. This capability, however, is not easy to achieve today because most enterprise deployments will start as a hybrid, possibly using a self-sovereign identity system for some verification processes and traditional identity access management and data collection systems for others. Data from an SSI system is then likely to make its way to the other system, leading to a loss of control by the holder when credential information and attributes are stored in enterprise systems. Interoperability with existing identity systems is important, however, because it will facilitate the gradual adoption of self-sovereign and decentralized identity structures. Self-Issued OpenID Provider (SIOP),[43] Credential Handler API

---

[43] "Section 7, Self-Issued OpenID," *OpenID Connect Core 1.0 Incorporating Errata Set 1,* https://openid.net/specs/openid-connect-core-1_0.html#SelfIssued.

(CHAPI),[44] and the OpenID Connect Credential Provider[45] represent some of the work being performed in this area.

One additional item to mention is privacy,[46] or rather the desire of a party to share credentials in such a way that their identity cannot be determined by other parties through correlation or information leakage. If correlation between credentials or attributes is possible, collusion may occur between participants in the trust triangle, leading to the identification of issuers, holders, or verifiers. The amount of anti-correlation support required is typically use case specific, with the level of privacy dependent on factors such as regulatory compliance. Regardless, the number of possible privacy violations is many, with examples provided as part of the Verifiable Credentials Data Model. Careful sharing of personally identifiable information, use of predicates, data minimization, short-lived identifiers, signature blinding,[47] pairwise identifiers, use of separate DIDs for separate relationships, and other techniques or best practices are recommended for increasing anti-correlation capabilities.

---

[44] Dave Longley and Manu Sporny, *Credential Handler API 1.0: Draft Community Group Report 23 June 2021*, https://w3c-ccg.github.io/credential-handler-api/.

[45] Tobias Looker et al., *OpenID Connect Credential Provider*, MATTR, April 20, 2021, https://mattrglobal.github.io/oidc-client-bound-assertions-spec/.

[46] Manu Sporny, Dave Longley, and David Chadwick, "Section 7: Privacy Considerations," *Verifiable Credentials Data Model v1.1*, (W3C Recommendation, March 3, 2022), https://w3c.github.io/vc-data-model/#privacy-considerations.

[47] Wikipedia, s.v. "Blind signature," last modified May 15, 2022, 18:10 (UTC), https://en.wikipedia.org/wiki/Blind_signature.

SELF-SOVEREIGN IDENTITY LANDSCAPE

Digital identity and the need to provide improved systems for individuals, organizations, and devices to share verified attributes and claims has recently grown. Accelerated by the global events of 2020–2021, and viewed as a key solution component for open banking, central bank digital currencies (CBDC), GDPR, health identifiers, cybersecurity, and others, active initiatives surrounding self-sovereign and decentralized identity have multiplied.

Some SSI capabilities, such as those positioned by Sovrin (https://sovrin.org/) and Evernym (https://www.evernym.com/), have been in the market for years. Related projects, such as Hyperledger Indy (https://www.hyperledger.org/projects/hyperledger-indy), Hyperledger Ursa (https://wiki.hyperledger.org/display/ursa/), and Hyperledger Aries (https://wiki.hyperledger.org/display/aries/) owe much of their creation to these earlier developments, with continued research largely community-led and open-source.

As the number of projects has grown, so have the consortiums and organizations focused on related global standards. The aforementioned W3C Credentials Community Group (https://www.w3.org/community/credentials/), Decentralized Identity Foundation (https://identity.foundation/), and the Linux Foundation (https://trustoverip.org/) are three organizations working on identity standards and specifications, with contributions from a number of industry leaders. IDunion (https://idunion.org/) is a new organization based on European values and regulations, with MOSIP (https://www.mosip.io/) and Verified.Me (https://verified.me/) also providing solutions for digital identity.

Initiatives such as the COVID Credentials Initiative (https://www.covidcreds.org/), IBM Digital Health Pass (https://www.ibm.com/products/digital-health-pass), and CommonPass (https://commonpass.org/) are more recent and driven by current global circumstances, with a focus on providing verified, digital credentials to support public health requirements.

IBM (https://www.ibm.com/blockchain/solutions/identity) and Microsoft (https://docs.microsoft.com/en-us/azure/active-directory/verifiable-credentials/) are active participants in this area, and even Stripe, the popular payments processing platform, is offering an identity service (https://stripe.com/en-ca/identity) for verifying identities via a set of exposed application APIs.

Finally, it is worth watching two other initiatives in this space. The first is the open-source ION project (https://github.com/decentralized-identity/ion) that is built around the Sidetree protocol (https://identity.foundation/sidetree/spec/). ION, contributed by Microsoft to the open-source community, is an implementation of Sidetree that allows decentralized identity operations to be anchored by the Bitcoin network without the need for centralized authorities, trusted third parties, tokens, or additional consensus methods. The Bitcoin network serves as a time-ordered anchor of hashes representing DID transaction batches, with the batches stored and managed by a content-addressable storage system (IPFS). This method allows a single on-chain transaction to represent thousands of transactions and provides Sidetree nodes with the information needed to create a consistent view of DIDs and DID Document states across the entire overlay network. The combination of external storage and the Bitcoin network improves performance while being fully open, public, and permissionless.

The second initiative is the Key Event Receipt Infrastructure (KERI) project (https://keri.one/), which takes digital identity architecture one step further by removing the need for an underlying public, global distributed ledger or blockchain. Based on the concepts of self-certifying identifiers (SCIDs) and key event logs, KERI enables DIDs (or any type of SCIDs) that are completely portable and not locked to any registry, DLT, or blockchain. The primary root of trust becomes the digital wallet alone, not a separate registry. The project itself is outlined in a detailed 130+ page whitepaper, so more details are definitely available. However, the flexibility, openness, scalability, interoperability, and advanced key management capabilities defined by KERI make it a project worth following.

It is impossible to list every company or organization in this area, with more surely to come. My recommendation is to start with the well-known standards bodies and their work, and then branch out to find the best technology that fits your needs. And expect some challenges and shortcomings with regard to interoperability because this area is rapidly evolving, with numerous options and ideas being presented.

EXTENDING IDENTITY BEYOND THE INDIVIDUAL

Organizational Identity

Individuals are not the only entities to which SSI concepts may be applied. Organizations also need a way to issue, hold, verify, and exchange trusted, secure, and private credentials and other information. Organizations may hold credentials in their own form of digital wallet (typically a secure cloud service) and issue verifiable credentials about themselves to other parties.

To address the problem of organizational identity, several consortiums and organizations have emerged. One commonly referenced example is the Verifiable Organizations Network (https://gcblockchain-chainedeblocsgc.github.io/verifiable-organization-network.html), a community formed by a couple of Canadian provincial governments. Built using a Hyperledger Indy-based network, this network provides a "searchable, public directory of open verifiable data about organizations."[48] Users access the network to obtain public verifiable credentials about a registered business, and other entities can use these VCs when determining whether

---

[48] "OrgBook BC: A Public Directory of Organizations Registered in BC," British Columbia official website, https://orgbook.gov.bc.ca/en/home.

to issue additional credentials (permits/licenses/registrations) to these businesses. This network replaces cumbersome, manual, and paper processes, and increases the trust, security, and privacy of the credentials. In public beta at the time of this writing, the Verifiable Organizations Network is one example of applying the concept of verifiable credentials to the real world.

Device Identity

The ability to trust the identity of devices providing data to enterprise systems is critical, especially when those devices are driving actions related to equipment operation, dangerous materials handling, autonomous vehicles, patient monitoring, or any number of use cases in which timely, accurate, and contextual information is important. If a device is compromised or impersonated, then decisions made based on the associated data cannot be trusted, and results can be catastrophic.

But scaling device identity services and building trust across IoT networks is complex. Devices are resource-constrained, distributed (often to remote locations), and heterogeneous. Some standards exist, but support can vary greatly, which makes interoperability between IoT networks difficult. Devices may attach to a gateway, which must be securely identified, and current identity models typically require devices to communicate to a centralized service, an issue if this service is compromised. Digital certificates, a common solution for securing devices today, also result in a maintenance problem because every device needs to have certificates generated, deployed, and kept up to date.

Although SSI is not widely used today to tackle these challenges, many of the concepts described in this chapter could be applied, depending on device type and context. For example:

- Wallets (hardware or software) could be incorporated into the device manufacturing process for devices with the capacity to support such components. These wallets could contain an embedded unique identifier, any generated key pairs, and be associated by the manufacturer via a DID to a verifiable data registry.

- Peer DIDs and DIDComm could be used to establish mutually authenticated and secure communication channels between devices, or between a device and another system or gateway.

- Verifiable credentials may be issued and presented to verify the manufacturer, metadata about a device, or to maintain a verified history of upgrades and maintenance.

ION could also support the registration of DIDs for IoT devices and be used to record associated IoT DID transactions against the Bitcoin network. And finally, KERI's lightweight approach to managing and replicating key events could increase IoT key management options and strengthen security guarantees.

These are just a few possibilities, with further work occurring in the community. Consortiums such as MOBI (https://dlt.mobi/) and the Industrial Internet Consortium (https://www.iiconsortium.org/), as well as organizations such as Chain of Things (https://www .chainofthings.com/) and Riddle & Code (https://www.riddleandcode .com/), are investigating the use of blockchain and SSI for problems related to device identity and management.

FINAL THOUGHTS

As the world shifts to become more digital, and as issues such as privacy, security, and fraud receive increased attention, the need for modern solutions to the problem of identity increases. Organizations must move to a "privacy by design"[49] mindset, where privacy is incorporated into applications, processes, and architectures by default. Government requirements such as GDPR and HIPAA, along with needed improvements in AML and KYC processes, also require an identity infrastructure designed to improve the customer experience while lowering costs and risk.

---

[49] Wikipedia, s.v. "Privacy by design," last modified March 26, 2022, 02:27, https://en.wikipedia.org/wiki/Privacy_by_design.

Distributed Identity Network (Blockchain)
Enables Peer to Peer Connectivity for the Purposes of Credential Verification
Auditable / Traceable, Secure Distributed Ledger, No Central Authority

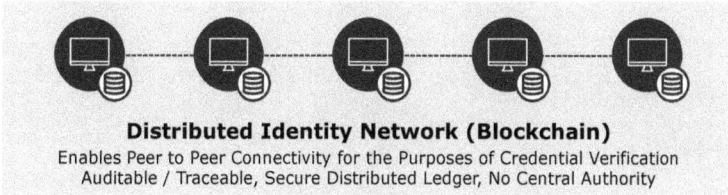

Decentralized identity model

Blockchain may address some but not all of the issues identified, a fact acknowledged by the complementary work being performed in this area. Other models exist, and in reality, the resulting solutions will likely consist of a combination of traditional and decentralized options. However, regardless of the approach, success will depend on several factors, including the ability to create platforms that are private, secure, and interoperable. A "one-size-fits-all" solution is not feasible, so the ability to decouple a subject's identity from the underlying infrastructure will be important to prevent lock-in, ensure portability, and shift control from a small number of organizations to the individual, organization, or device. It's a fascinating area, with the potential to positively influence how we interact in the digital world. I personally look forward to watching the possibilities unfold.

Chapter 9

BLOCKCHAIN AND PRIVACY

Throughout this book, transaction confidentiality and privacy have been discussed as core considerations for enterprise blockchain applications. The need for privacy to protect the identity of an individual or organization, and confidentiality to secure transactional data, figures in many enterprise use cases including finance, healthcare, and retail. Privacy and confidentiality answer the question: "Who has access to what data?" and ensures that only the information and identities needed for a decision are shared or exchanged between parties. The terms "confidentiality and privacy" are often used interchangeably in everyday conversation, and for simplicity I will often do the same in this chapter, but be aware that from a legal standpoint, the terms are separate and distinct.

Confidentiality and privacy are also key elements of trust. Without them, individuals and organizations wouldn't trust each other or the products and services offered. Yahoo, Facebook, LinkedIn, and Equifax are just a few companies that did not maintain appropriate data privacy and confidentiality controls in the past, and as a result data was compromised and consumer trust negatively affected.

But how do you build confidentiality and privacy capabilities into an enterprise? Incorporating privacy in a centralized architecture is simple in theory: place responsibility in the hands of a single authority who stores and selectively reveals data to authorized parties. However, as discussed, centralization of data and business logic have their own issues, including the need to completely trust the designated authority, a loss of control, and exposure of a single attack vector to malicious third parties. Auditability is an additional challenge because the authority responsible for ensuring confidentiality and privacy is then also responsible for tracking it, an obvious conflict of interest in many circumstances.

In this chapter, I describe the role of blockchain and other related technologies in building confidentiality, privacy, and integrity into a distributed, decentralized architecture. The exact privacy features supported by blockchain frameworks differ greatly, including the choices of consensus algorithm, smart contract capabilities, private data support, key management, and support for features such as zero-knowledge proofs. Regardless, it is important to be aware of the technologies and protocols emerging as potential solutions, and their fit into the enterprise landscape.

MULTI-SIG AND SECURE MULTI-PARTY COMPUTING

To start, it is useful to briefly introduce two concepts that serve as the basis for many emerging security, privacy, and confidentiality solutions: multi-sig (multi-signatures) and secure multi-party computing (MPC).

Multi-sig is a scheme requiring multiple digital signatures to be associated with a blockchain transaction upon submission. For example, in the cryptocurrency world, a multi-sig wallet can require signatures from "2 of 3" parties, a threshold established on wallet creation. Initially made popular as a way to enhance security for Bitcoin transactions, multi-sig wallets can now be used to secure various types of cryptocurrencies, as well as smart contract transactions exposed by networks such as Ethereum.

However, even though multi-sig can improve security, it has limitations. It may actually reduce privacy and confidentiality because multiple entities are now potentially aware of the transaction and its associated data. It uses rigid approval policies and static keys that may eventually be compromised and introduces dependencies on a particular ledger.

These weaknesses have led to growing research in applying secure multi-party computation (MPC) to crypto wallets, which are designed to tackle multi-sig shortcomings and improve security. With MPC, the private key used to sign a blockchain transaction is

derived from multiple fragments or shares distributed across multiple parties. Each party is unaware of the other's fragments, there
is no need for each party to own and manage a separate private key
(unlike multi-sig), and the result (a digitally signed transaction) is
collectively generated. The MPC operates off-chain, which improves
performance, makes the transaction size smaller, and the corresponding network fees lower. Plus, the result is not tied to a particular blockchain framework. MPC has yet to be widely adopted in the
cryptocurrency community, but it shows promise for increasing the
security and flexibility of cryptocurrency blockchain transactions.

But MPC can be used for more than just private key creation and
cryptocurrency transactions. It also shows promise for use cases
needing multiple parties to collaborate on the analysis of confidential data without compromising its security and privacy. For example, hospitals could share data to improve detection and treatment
of illnesses. Currently, the need for personal medical data to stay
private makes sharing it for analysis difficult if not impossible. MPC
protocols and cryptographic techniques would allow hospitals to
retain data privacy and still support computations against it. Input
data would not be shared; only the results of the MPC would be
revealed. As the use of AI/ML grows, and as the need for more data
accelerates, the ability to analyze data while maintaining privacy
and confidentiality will become increasingly critical.

However, MPC in this context still has several challenges, including performance and functional limitations, and the possibility of

input data leakage, where the protocol and its output "leaks" information about the input data. Complementary privacy-preserving approaches to MPC are under development, such as federated learning, homomorphic encryption, and trusted execution environments (TEE). And, as we shall see, while each of these does not necessarily involve blockchain, there is an opportunity for blockchain to play an expanded role as organizations attempt to gain more value from data while meeting privacy, security, confidentiality, and regulatory requirements.

ZERO-KNOWLEDGE PROOFS (ZKPS)

No discussion on privacy and confidentiality would be complete without mentioning zero-knowledge proofs (ZKP) and associated concepts such as PLONK, zk-SNARKS, zk-STARKS, zk-Rollups, Bulletproofs, and homomorphic encryption.[50] While a full deep dive on these concepts would require pages of complex math and numerous computer science courses, it is important to introduce these topics and their potential relevance in enterprise use cases such as anti-money laundering/know-your-customer (AML/KYC), payments, medical record management, digital identity, and others.

To start, it is often stated that a true ZKP needs to prove three criteria[51]:

---

[50] The list of acronyms seemingly never ends! There are many others.

[51] Wikipedia, s.v. "Zero-knowledge proof," last modified June 2, 2022, 15:27 (UTC), https://en.wikipedia.org/wiki/Zero-knowledge_proof.

1. **Completeness:** If the statement is true, the honest verifier (that is, one following the protocol properly) will be convinced of this fact by an honest prover.

2. **Soundness:** If the statement is false, no cheating prover can convince the honest verifier that it is true, except with some small probability.

3. **Zero knowledge:** If the statement is true, no verifier learns anything other than the fact that the statement is true.

These points will become clearer as we look at some examples, but generally, as mentioned in Chapter 3, ZKPs allow parties to prove they possess a certain fact or secret without actually revealing that fact or secret.

One example used in technology circles to describe the concept is the Ali Baba cave[52] story. In this story, Peggy (the prover of the statement) proves to Victor (the verifier) that she knows a secret word that activates a magic door without actually revealing the secret word. This proof is done through a series of rounds or interactions, which eventually lead to Victor being convinced of Peggy's knowledge. In ZKP, this type of proof is referred to as an interactive

---

[52] Jean-Jacques Quisquater et al., "How to Explain Zero-Knowledge Protocols to Your Children: The Strange Cave of Ali Baba," (Conference paper, Advances in Cryptology – CRYPTO '89, Santa Barbara, CA, August 1989), http://dx.doi.org/10.1007/0-387-34805-0_60.

ZKP, as the prover and verifier interact with one another as part of the protocol.

For other examples, refer to the discussion on ZKPs in Chapter 8 for selective disclosure, predicate generation (age > 21), or the creation of derived verifiable credentials without revealing the details behind the credentials. As in the Ali Baba cave example, privacy and confidentiality are maintained during these identity generation and verification processes; the prover is able to prove to a verifier that a statement is true without revealing any additional details.

Zero-knowledge proofs are a very powerful concept, providing organizations with the ability to preserve data privacy and confidentiality in blockchain and non-blockchain contexts. An ongoing area of research, ZKPs were actually first made popular in the blockchain community by organizations such as Zcash (https://z.cash/) that were looking to increase privacy for ledger-based financial transactions. Unlike other blockchain networks, which expose full transaction details, Zcash provides selectable support for shielded addresses. Transactions between these addresses are encrypted on the Zcash network (thus hiding the transaction details from other parties) but may still be verified through the use of a special form of zero-knowledge proofs called Succinct Non-interactive Arguments of Knowledge (zk-SNARKS).

zk-SNARKS are a type of non-interactive zero-knowledge proof (NIZK). These proofs, which do require a setup phase, allow proof verification to take place independently from proof creation because little to no interaction between the prover and verifier is involved. With zk-SNARKS, the prover calculates a proof, which is made available to a verifier. The verifier can then separately verify the proof and be convinced of the prover's claim. The proofs are succinct, in that they can be quickly verified, and "arguments of knowledge" because they meet the soundness criteria.

There are many types of ZKPs, each with different optimizations and trade-offs. Certain ZKPs focus on the efficiency of the prover (prover times), while others focus on the verifier (verification times). Bulletproofs and Scalable Transparent ARguments of Knowledge (zk-STARKS) support trustless setup, which is the approach researched by networks such as Monero (https://www.getmonero .org/resources/moneropedia/bulletproofs.html) for transaction privacy (range proofs). And to address concerns about performance, networks such as Ethereum are looking at bundling or rolling up groups of transactions executed outside of the main Ethereum layer (on a Layer 2 protocol) and then posted to the main layer (Layer 1). This bundling takes the form of a cryptographic proof referred to as zero-knowledge rollups (zk-rollups), where thousands of transactions may be rolled up into a single proof. StarkWare (https:// starkware.co/) and ImmutableX (https://www.immutable.com/) are examples of networks that provide a Layer 2 network and zk-rollups on top of the main Ethereum (Layer 1) network.

Zero-knowledge proofs, while likely to be broadly deployed for financial and DeFi use cases as a way to verify transactions, offer future potential for enterprise use cases needing privacy and audit-ability in a public or shared decentralized system. I discuss the possible use of ZKPs for managing private data later in this chapter, and you can expect further developments in this area for scenarios requiring data privacy and confidentiality.

PRIVACY, ENCRYPTION, AND TRUSTED EXECUTION ENVIRONMENTS

As discussed, ZKPs are extremely useful for proving something is true without revealing any additional information about the inputs behind the proof. However, these proofs do not secure data while it is being processed—they only address the inputs and outcome. Approaches that secure data while it is being stored (encryption) or moved across a network (TLS) are also not sufficient. For scenarios requiring data or code privacy during execution, alternatives are required. In this chapter, I look at two: homomorphic encryption and the use of secure enclaves or trusted execution environments (TEEs).

Homomorphic encryption allows software-based computations to be performed against encrypted data, thus maintaining the data's privacy and confidentiality. Encrypted data is sent to a software service where calculations or other forms of processing are per-formed without any form of decryption. The result is identical to that achieved against unencrypted data (given the same inputs). Relatively early for enterprise applicability and adoption due to issues related to performance, homomorphic encryption is worth watching as a potential solution to the problem of secure execution on data.

The second method uses hardware to support the creation of secure enclaves or trusted execution environments (TEEs). These environments provide application developers with an isolated, protected enclave or memory space that is separate from the rest of the compute infrastructure. Data or code running in these enclaves is fully segmented and protected. The authenticity of the code in the enclave may be cryptographically proven, and access by outside applications, users, or processes is prevented. Solutions such as Intel's Software Guard Extensions (Intel SGX) or AMD's Secure Technology use this approach, and public cloud providers such as Azure, AWS, and Google offer various options for instantiating trusted execution environments within applications, containers, or virtual machines.

The concept of a secure enclave or TEE is not new; vendors such as Apple include secure enclaves on devices such as iPhones and Macs to store and control access to private keys. However, recent work has combined these environments with blockchain to secure blockchain transactions and data during processing, or to support off-chain or external processing. For example, Hyperledger's Avalon (https://github.com/hyperledger/avalon) project, a solution I will cover further in Chapter 10, demonstrates how Intel SGX and blockchain can be used to support trusted off-chain computation and attested oracles.

Microsoft Azure's Confidential Ledger (in preview at the time of this writing; https://azure.microsoft.com/en-ca/services/azure-confidential-ledger/) leverages TEEs with blockchain and DLTs for managing data. Further, R3 has announced it is working with IBM (https://www.r3.com/blog/corda-enterprise-on-ibm-linuxone/) on a secure environment for Corda Enterprise. There is also related work occurring in the technology community, including through the Linux Foundation Confidential Computing Consortium (https://confiden tialcomputing.io/), Confidential Consortium Framework (https://github.com/microsoft/CCF), and the Enterprise Ethereum Alliance Off-Chain Trusted Compute Specification (https://entethalliance.github.io/trusted-computing/spec.html).

As data becomes more critical to organizations, and as emphasis is placed on the privacy, confidentiality, and integrity of the data and associated computations, the use of encryption, secure enclaves, and trusted execution environments is likely to grow. Blockchain can play a critical role in these environments, something I cover further in Chapter 10.

MANAGING PRIVATE DATA IN BLOCKCHAIN

Multi-sig, MPC, trusted execution environments, advanced cryptography, and zero-knowledge proofs all have the potential to play a key role in maintaining data privacy and confidentiality. However, there are other options to be aware of, especially for enterprises deploying blockchain solutions today.

One option involves the use of on-chain encryption. In this case, data stored in a blockchain network (typically a permissioned or consortium network) is encrypted such that it can only be accessed by the targeted participants. Although relatively simple to implement, this approach raises several concerns. If a key is compromised, the entire network is open to attack and unwanted data exposure may result. Data sovereignty can also be an issue because even encrypted data can be considered by legal entities as restricted and thus cannot leave a specific country or jurisdiction. Techniques such as key rotation and forward secrecy[53] may help alleviate some of these concerns, but inevitably the amount of acceptable risk will be determined by the nature of the blockchain network.

A second option is to selectively distribute data to participants across a blockchain network. This capability allows data to be delivered and viewable to only those participants involved in the transaction. Hyperledger Fabric, for example, supports defining private data collections[54] in addition to channels[55] to provide private data sharing or direct communication paths between network members. R3's Corda platform provides partial visibility of transactions (only the nodes involved in a transaction encounter the transaction), with other blockchain platforms offering similar features. While not

---

[53] Wikipedia, s.v. "Forward secrecy," last modified May 23, 2022, 10:20 (UTC), https://en.wikipedia.org/wiki/Forward_secrecy.

[54] "Private Data," Hyperledger Documentation, https://hyperledger-fabric.readthedocs.io/en/release-2.2/private-data/private-data.html.

[55] "Channels," Hyperledger Documentation, https://hyperledger-fabric.readthedocs.io/en/release-2.2/channels.html.

relevant in a public blockchain context, this approach can be useful for networks in which the participants are known, and not all data needs to be shared with everyone. However, these capabilities tend to be platform-specific, and thus not shareable across blockchain frameworks. They can also be difficult to manage and administer, especially if the number of participants, communication paths, and transaction types is fairly large and diverse.

A third option, briefly covered in Chapter 5, is to store sensitive data off-chain while retaining a reference to this data on a blockchain network. In this case, blockchain transactions contain a hash of the actual data (a "pointer"), while the data itself is stored in an external storage technology. If, upon retrieval, the blockchain and stored data hashes do not match, then an investigation as to why the data or hashes are different needs to be undertaken. Access to the off-chain data can be controlled through common authn/ authz techniques, with further controls implemented through smart contracts. It can be argued that this method introduces the need to trust an external third party, namely the owner of the off-chain data store, and requires the blockchain network to be used in conjunction with another technology. Regardless, this means of decentralizing privacy has been outlined in a number of papers,[56] along with various options for improving overall privacy and confidentiality through ZKPs, MPC, and other techniques. As always,

[56] Guy Zyskind, Oz Nathan, and Alex Pentland, "Decentralizing Privacy: Using Blockchain to Protect Personal Data" (2015 IEEE Security and Privacy Workshops), 180–184, https://www.doi.org/10.1109/SPW.2015.27.

carefully consider the requirements and trade-offs when applying this solution to the enterprise.

Lastly, as defined in Chapter 3, oracles may be used to improve the security of externally referenced data, state channels (described in the next section) to keep transactions off-chain and exclusive between parties, and application-specific networks to limit the data types and participants to a specific domain. These approaches can also increase the security and privacy of data across a blockchain network.

PRIVACY AND SMART CONTRACTS

One final element of privacy and confidentiality involves processing transaction data in the context of blockchain smart contracts. As covered in Chapter 6, many blockchain frameworks, such as Ethereum, store and execute smart contracts in a public context. The underlying code and state are visible by anyone, as are all inputs and outputs. This transparency can be beneficial for reasons already discussed, but it introduces complexity when maintaining privacy and confidentiality in the enterprise.

To address these concerns, some of the methods covered in this chapter can be applied to smart contracts, with popular blockchain frameworks including features for securing smart contract execution. For example, Hyperledger Fabric has introduced the concept of private chaincode (https://github.com/hyperledger

/fabric-private-chaincode), which enables execution of Fabric smart contracts within enclaves in an Intel SGX trusted execution environment.

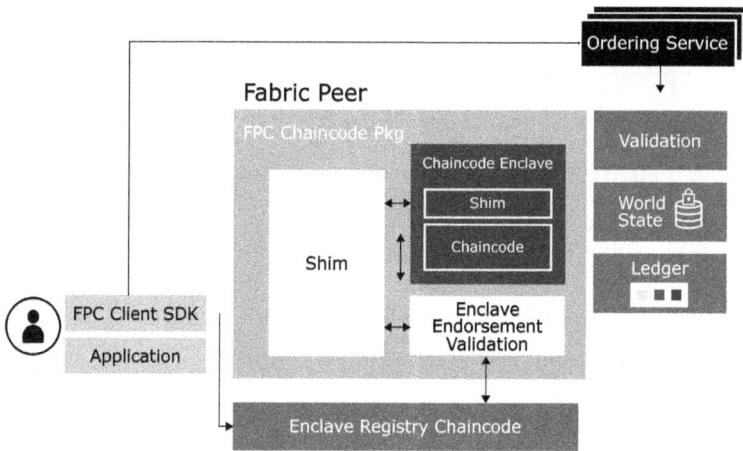

Hyperledger Fabric Private Chaincode architecture[57]

Chaincode runs in an enclave that is isolated from the peer and other chaincode; state encryption, attestation, and secure blockchain state access are provided. Peers and clients are also able to verify that a specific smart contract executes in an actual enclave. This model protects the privacy of chaincode data and computation from potentially untrusted peers.

[57] Hyperledger, Fabric Private Chaincode documentation and codebase on GitHub, https://github.com/hyperledger/fabric-private-chaincode.

Other blockchain networks such as the Secret Network (https://scrt
.network/) provide data privacy and confidentiality by "...allowing
decentralized applications to perform encrypted computations.
Secret Contracts can take encrypted inputs and produce encrypted
outputs, without exposing any data while it is in use. In addition,
contract state remains encrypted throughout executions."[58] As with
other privacy-centric solutions, data privacy in the Secret Network
is achieved through keys, encryption protocols, and a trusted execution environment. The code remains public for transparency
purposes, but the data is secured.

Other options for improving the security of smart contract execution and data privacy include the use of state channels (where
transactions between parties are directly executed over off-chain
channels and only the starting and closing transactions are written
to the blockchain), hashed timelock agreements (where recipients
cryptographically acknowledge a transaction within a certain time
period), and private smart contract systems such as Hawk.[59] At
the time of this writing, most of these options are in the very early
stages of development and deployment, so expect a number of
advancements in the future.

---

[58] "What is Secret Network?" Secret Network documentation,
https://build.scrt.network/overview.html.

[59] Ahmed Kosba et al., "Hawk: The Blockchain Model of Cryptography and Privacy-
Preserving Smart Contracts," (2016 IEEE Symposium on Security and Privacy (SP)),
839-858, https://doi.org/10.1109/SP.2016.55.

FINAL THOUGHTS

Privacy and confidentiality are hot topics in the enterprise. Vast amounts of data, the need to collect or synthetically generate more data for improved AI/ML model accuracy, a desire to build broader decentralized business networks, and increased regulatory and individual concerns about personal information management and ownership are all driving advancements in this area. And while various approaches have been in the cryptocurrency and public blockchain space for quite some time, the use of technologies such as ZKPs and trusted execution environments in the enterprise is only recently gaining traction.

Hopefully this chapter has served as a great starting point for you, and brought clarity to various terms and concepts associated with this complex area. It also sets the foundation for our next subject, the role of blockchain in enterprise architectures.

Chapter 10

BLOCKCHAIN IN ENTERPRISE ARCHITECTURES

We've covered several blockchain-related topics up to this point, and now it's time to bring them together and provide examples of where they might fit in an enterprise IT landscape.

Enterprises today have mainframes, legacy systems, volumes of data, hybrid cloud environments, security concerns, complex processes, and various other technical challenges. Where and how can blockchain be applied? What do the resulting architectures look like? How are the right levels of performance, scalability, security, and governance achieved? And how do you determine if a blockchain is even needed?

This chapter attempts to answer these questions by looking at blockchain technology in enterprise architecture patterns without yet involving cryptocurrency or tokenization. Chapter 11 will address tokens and the associated digital products that will become important to the enterprise in the near future, but there are important architectural considerations to address beyond tokenization, which this chapter covers.

It is impossible to discuss every architectural pattern or scenario, but each of the general patterns covered here can be used in various use cases, many of which were introduced in Chapter 2. After some examples, this chapter ends with a discussion important not only to blockchain, but also to the use of all technology: understanding if the technology is a fit, alternatives, and criteria that would help with the decision.

STATE OF THE MARKET

First, a recap of the state and direction of the enterprise blockchain market is important. At this writing, blockchain in many ways remains an overloaded and misunderstood term. Marketing literature often labels vendor solutions as "blockchain" regardless of the number of blockchain elements actually included. Unrealistic promises of business value are made, and many non-technical success factors—such as required legal frameworks, consortium governance models, organizational structures, business model transitions, and regulatory changes—are glossed over or ignored.

Despite the hype, blockchain is in the early stages of development. Today's enterprise blockchain deployments provide value but are often used to simply improve a business process or streamline data collection and distribution, solutions that may not need blockchain capabilities at all. However, as the world shifts to creating a new internet of value incorporating capabilities such as DAOs, dApps, self-sovereign identity (SSI), digital products and assets, and others, the extent to which blockchain becomes the core foundation of complete business solutions will increase.

In the future, distributed ledgers, decentralization, consensus, smart contracts, encryption, trust, SSI, and tokenization are likely to become a part of any solution described as "blockchain," with optional add-ons such as AI/ML or the Internet of Things (IoT) enhancing the solution. Deployments will span multiple organizations, regulatory guidelines will adjust, and the value of the technology will increase as blockchain becomes a more integrated component, or even replaces several components within the enterprise. This picture aligns with the discussion in Chapter 1, where I described today's highly connected interactions, decentralized business networks, and the need to innovate and collaborate. Add tokenization, and you have a future world with new business models; programmable, digital products and assets; and decentralized or autonomous decision-making.

It will take some time for these solutions to evolve, and for non-technical factors, such as organizational structure and culture, to catch up and align with new approaches and business models. I dig further into the future of blockchain in Chapter 12. Here, the focus is blockchain in current enterprise architectures, and how it can be used to augment many of today's technologies and practices.

THE STACK DIAGRAM

Regardless of how blockchain evolves, and the extent to which solutions are built on the technology, organizations will still need to support certain core IT functions and requirements. These include the need to integrate with legacy systems; handle batch and real-time data; derive insights from data via analytics; incorporate IoT devices; streamline and secure identity; manage, secure, and govern data; and more. Blockchain will not exist in a vacuum; it will not only have to interoperate with other blockchain networks, but also with any number of technologies within an IT landscape. This includes newly built or deployed cloud applications that will, of course, also become legacy at some point.

To meet these needs, it is useful to place blockchain in the context of these core functions and requirements. I've added the diagram below as one example of how blockchain can be used with commonly deployed enterprise technologies. The blockchain components, as well as identity and edge processing/IoT, have already been covered in this book, so I will provide a description of the other elements to clarify their role with blockchain. Besides, every technology book needs a good stack diagram!

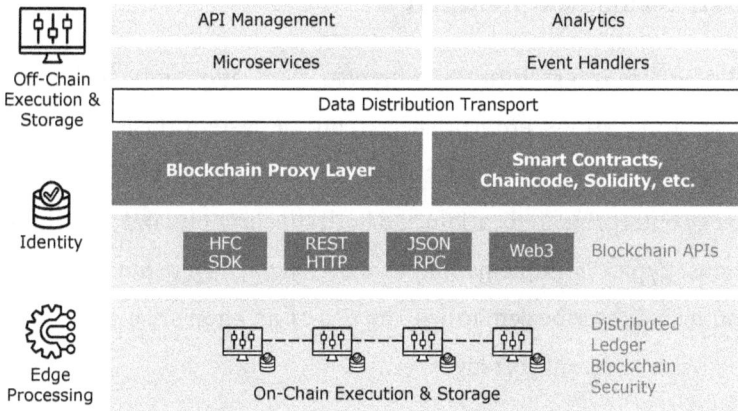

Blockchain will live alongside other architectural elements.

Blockchain Proxy Layer

A blockchain proxy layer creates a level of abstraction between the underlying core blockchain technology stack and integrated applications or services. When communicating via this layer, all blockchains look the same, reducing the level of dependency on the selected technology and allowing for decoupled solution architectures. Note that given the state of today's blockchain technology stacks, it can be difficult to achieve a completely generic proxy layer because capabilities and approaches often vary greatly between solutions. However, the use of system-level microservices that bundle commonly used blockchain features into generic APIs can facilitate creation of such a proxy layer.

Data Distribution Transport

Blockchain interactions may involve many endpoints, including user applications, enterprise systems, or system/business APIs. Interactions may be bi-directional (initiated by the blockchain or by an enterprise application) and both synchronous and asynchronous. Typically implemented as a messaging layer that supports publish-subscribe semantics, the use of an enterprise-scale data distribution transport layer can:

- Improve endpoint location independence

- Increase the ability of the architecture to scale (both in data volume and number of endpoints)

- Guarantee message delivery

- Reduce the overhead associated with polling or pure request/reply systems

The data distribution transport often also forms the basis of an event-driven blockchain architecture.

Microservices and Automation

Microservices and automation capabilities (such as workflow, robotic process automation/RPA, or case management) are typically used to implement the enterprise business services that will use the blockchain layer for establishing a business network—or for incorporating other blockchain-related capabilities into defined business logic. While a complete discussion on microservices and automation is beyond the scope of this book, it is important to consider the strategies and patterns used to create and deploy business services within an enterprise architecture, and to consider the technical, operational (DevOps) and organizational aspects.[60]

Event Handlers

Event handlers are components configured to listen for changes to the blockchain or the connected endpoints, and to automatically invoke appropriate enterprise logic in response to these changes. For example, event handlers may receive notification via a callback of a new transaction on the ledger or a message from a connected enterprise application via the data distribution transport. Event handlers typically work in conjunction with blockchain APIs and the data distribution transport, and may be bundled or created as microservices within the enterprise architecture. They also facilitate creation of the event-driven architecture mentioned previously.

---

[60] "Conway's Law," website of Mel Conway,
http://www.melconway.com/Home/Conways_Law.html.

API Management

APIs drive the ease with which applications can share information both inside and outside the firewall. As blockchain capabilities are deployed within and across enterprises, and as levels of abstraction are defined (via a proxy layer, event handlers, or microservices/automation), it will become important to control and manage access to business-level APIs—those that subsequently access system or low-level blockchain APIs. To do so, an API gateway or broader API management platform can be used.

This layer allows an enterprise to:

- Define security capabilities independent of the services themselves

- Expose APIs as products, for example, for use by third-party developers

- Control API contracts

- Obtain visibility into the performance and use of APIs

APIs can also provide access to the data (transactions) within the blockchain, again via well-defined interfaces and security controls.

Analytics

As a blockchain is deployed across a business network, and as transactions are added to the distributed ledger, the blockchain will soon contain (or reference) a large amount of extremely valuable information.

- How can a business make use of this information (assuming appropriate security and visibility) to improve business decisions?

- How can events (transactions) sent to/received from the blockchain be viewed immediately (for example, in the case of attempted fraud) without waiting for batch-style reports to be delivered?

- How can the results of automated business transactions and processes be analyzed for identifying process improvements, detecting SLA violations, or conforming to regulatory requirements?

An analytics layer can be used to answer these types of questions. Within the strict security guidelines of the implemented blockchain technology stack (and typically via secured APIs), users can access, view, and analyze state and transaction data (both in batch and real-time) to identify threats or opportunities in the network.

Off-chain Execution and Storage

As described in chapters 5 and 9, any blockchain implementation will require an analysis of what should be done on-chain vs. off-chain. Trade-offs need to be considered, including storage requirements, overall blockchain size, performance, block size limits, data longevity/durability requirements, smart contract access to off-chain content, and the need for a globally consistent state. Identified storage requirements may also help determine if a blockchain is truly needed, or if alternative storage like IPFS or AWS QLDB is sufficient for the use case.

There are many ways that a stack diagram like this can be drawn, with many levels of detail under each layer such as security controls, IAM strategies, storage technologies, ERP systems, container management frameworks, networking technologies, and cloud platforms. You will inevitably find each of these layers present in almost every enterprise, regardless of the vertical. The key point to remember is that for blockchain to be successful, it cannot exist alone.

There are various options for making it easier to incorporate blockchain, at least in its current form. You can manually install, configure, and manage a blockchain stack in an environment you control, which provides the most flexibility, but can be challenging to maintain given the rapid pace of technology change. Remember that, for a permissioned or consortium network, deployment applies to not just one organization, but to all participating organizations, which increases the level of complexity and coordination required.

Alternatively, various vendors and cloud providers provide block-chain "as a service," where either the core platform or a pre-built solution is available typically in a cloud environment. This makes the solution easier to use and consume but can potentially lock you into a particular technology framework and put you at the mercy of the vendor for upgrades, security, and enhancements. As with anything, trade-offs exist, and it is important to weigh each factor carefully when developing your blockchain strategy and adoption style.

BLOCKCHAIN AND DATA MANAGEMENT

Data is a critical element and differentiator for enterprises today. The organization that generates the most value from its data has a huge advantage in the marketplace and is often the organization that survives under difficult circumstances. However, the challenges surrounding data are immense, with concerns such as its collection, security, quality, analysis, distribution, and delivery all sharing the limelight with enterprise data strategies and priorities.

Blockchain may not solve all data issues, but it can play a role in improving various aspects of the data processing puzzle, including data collection, security, integrity, and analytics. I've included some examples in the following sections, with more likely to emerge as blockchain technology and related data handling strategies mature.

Data Collection

Data collection is the obvious first step in any data processing pipeline. Data must be collected accurately from trusted sources to achieve the best results. It must be captured at the speed it is generated, including large volumes of real-time data from IoT sensors or batch data from a file. And it needs to be made available to downstream processes quickly and in context to realize maximum value.

Data collection capabilities and associated trust and quality measures are critical to any organization. This is especially true of a blockchain. Just because data is on a blockchain network doesn't mean it's accurate! If bad data is not caught before it's processed by a smart contract or added to an underlying ledger, the blockchain network will be more than happy to distribute this bad data to all participants.

To aid in the collection of data, whether storing it on- or off-chain, many of the blockchain features discussed in this book can be used. Smart contracts can include data validation checks to catch bad data before it is written to the underlying ledger, oracles can be used to ensure externally accessed data is trustworthy and accurate, and various identity techniques can be employed to verify that data is coming from a trusted source, whether a third-party, external system, or IoT device. Underlying DLTs and consensus algorithms can ensure all parties have an agreed-upon copy of the data, and cryptography with hashing can be used to write provenance records to the network for auditing or data tracing. These techniques can be combined with external or off-chain data collection processes, storage technologies, or analyses to facilitate development and maintenance of trusted, governed, and auditable collection processes.

Again, blockchain will not operate in a vacuum. Components such as event listeners, APIs, data services, and transformations will co-exist with a blockchain deployment to facilitate collection of both batch and real-time data from a variety of sources. It is also possible to treat blockchain as a data source itself, as shown in the following diagram.

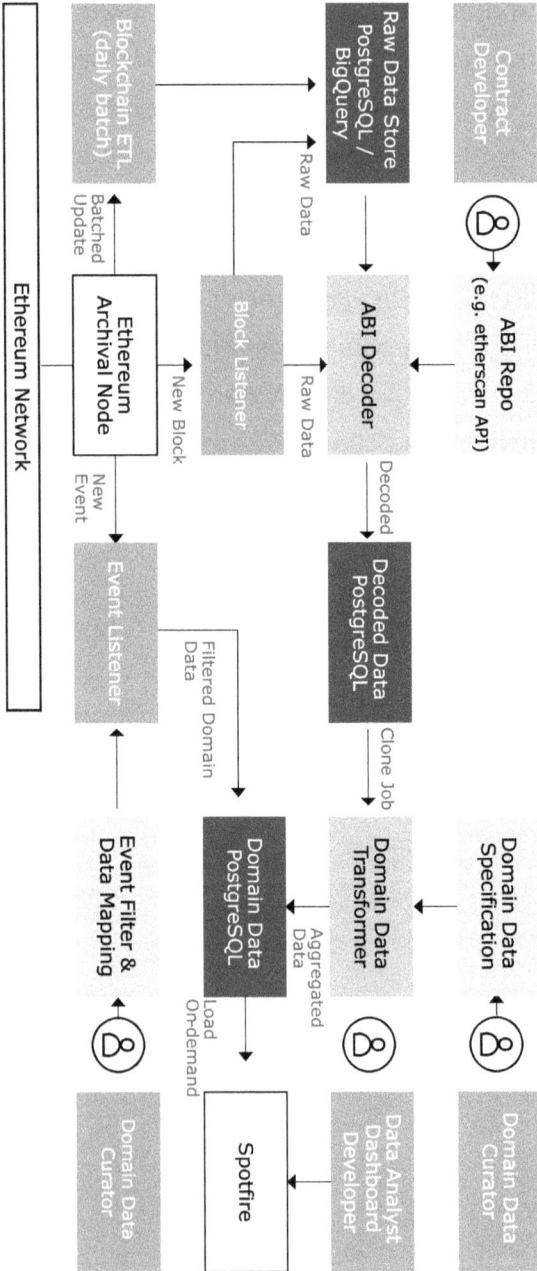

Example of Ethereum data capture for analytics

In this example, events generated by a blockchain network such as Ethereum may be received by listeners configured to monitor certain transactions or smart contracts. Upon receipt of an event, transformers can use metadata from an associated application binary interface (ABI), for example, to decode the event data and forward the results to a storage technology for use by other applications or systems. Audit information can be added to track the source of the data, and hashes can be checked on subsequent reads to ensure the externally stored data matches the data on the ledger. This processing model is almost certain to become more common in the enterprise as the use of blockchain grows, the amount of data on public and permissioned networks increases, and the need to include this data in operational decisions becomes necessary.

Data Integrity, Privacy, and Security

Beyond the capabilities incorporated during data collection, blockchain and related technologies can offer additional data integrity, privacy, confidentiality, and security features. As mentioned in Chapter 9, zero-knowledge proofs (ZKPs), on-chain encryption, private data channels, and hashing can be used to increase the security, privacy, and trust of any data stored or referenced by a blockchain network. The tamper-resistant ledger elevates the level of trust of any stored data, and the distributed network increases data availability.

These features are all extremely useful as organizations increasingly attempt to answer questions such as:

- What is the original source of my data?

- Has any of my data been tampered with or altered?

- Who is using my data?

- How do I prove I am managing my data according to regulatory guidelines?

- Is any of my sensitive data managed or controlled by a single individual or authority?

- What risk does data centralization introduce into my business?

Further developments in areas such as homomorphic encryption and ZKPs will also enable organizations to improve their data integrity, security, and trustworthiness—especially in deployments involving multiple partners or participants.

Analytics and Data Processing

After collecting and storing data in a form that is secure, governed, and verified, it now must be made available to processes for decision-making. However, the need to maintain appropriate confidentiality and privacy, as discussed in Chapter 9, extends beyond encrypting data on the network or in a database. In certain use cases, data also needs to be secured while it is being processed, which is driving research in areas such as homomorphic encryption (processing data while it is encrypted) and the use of trusted execution environments (TEEs).

As previously mentioned, homomorphic encryption is relatively new and has yet to receive broad adoption in the enterprise. However, it is worth covering TEEs in more detail because this capability is available to enterprises today in various forms, from cloud vendor services to open-source projects. To review it, I will use the open source Hyperledger Avalon (https://github.com/hyperledger/avalon) project as one example of a framework that combines Intel SGX and blockchain to support trusted off-chain computation.

Enterprise 1	Enterprise 2		Enterprise N
Requestors	Requestors	● ● ●	Requestors
Enterprise 1 Blockchain Node	Enterprise 2 Blockchain Node	*Enterprise Blockchain Network*	Enterprise N Blockchain Node
Off-chain Trusted Compute Service	Off-chain Trusted Compute Service		Off-chain Trusted Compute Service
Trusted Worker	Trusted Worker		Trusted Worker

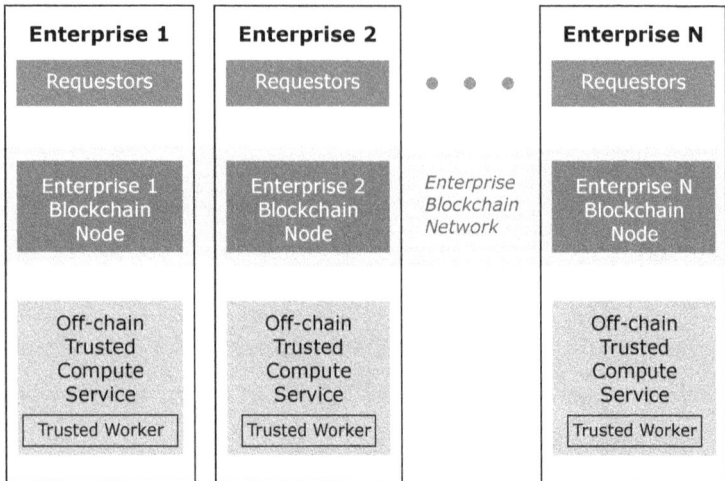

Hyperledger Avalon system overview[61]

Hyperledger Avalon is based on the principles of the Enterprise Ethereum Alliance Off-Chain Trusted Compute Specification and moves resource-intensive processing from on-chain to off-chain "workers" that run in a trusted execution environment. On-chain capabilities remain, but instead of processing data, these capabilities[62] are used to:

---

[61] "Hyperledger Avalon Architecture Overview, Revision 0.3," Hyperledger documentation on GitHub, found at https://github.com/hyperledger/avalon/tree/main/docs.

[62] Hyperledger, hyperledger/avalon documentation and codebase on GitHub, https://github.com/hyperledger/avalon.

- Maintain a registry of trusted workers

- Provide work order submissions from a client(s) to a worker

- Preserve a log of work order receipts and acknowledgments

The policies and metadata associated with each of the submitted requests is managed on-chain, while off-chain workers handle the heavy-lifting in combination with TEEs such as Intel SGX. Requestors and workers are registered on the blockchain, and requestors submit work orders to the network for processing by the underlying workers. Requests may be handled by any worker (regardless of the enterprise hosting that worker), and all interactions are written back to the blockchain network to build a complete audit trail.

Blockchain

Avalon Connector Library Requester App (UI, script)

Smart Contracts
- Worker Registry
- Work Order Queue
- Work Order Receipts

Trusted Compute Service

HTTP/JSON RPC Listener

Blockchain Connector

Orchestration

WorkerWorker Avalon Microservice (Container)

Key Management Enclave

Work Order Processing Enclave

Workload

Scripts, Models, Data

Inside-Out API

Worker Registry and Work Order Queue Manager

Work Order Queue

Work Order Registry

Other Workers (TrustZone, ZKP, MPC)

External Data Source

Reusable Avalon framework   Custom app specific

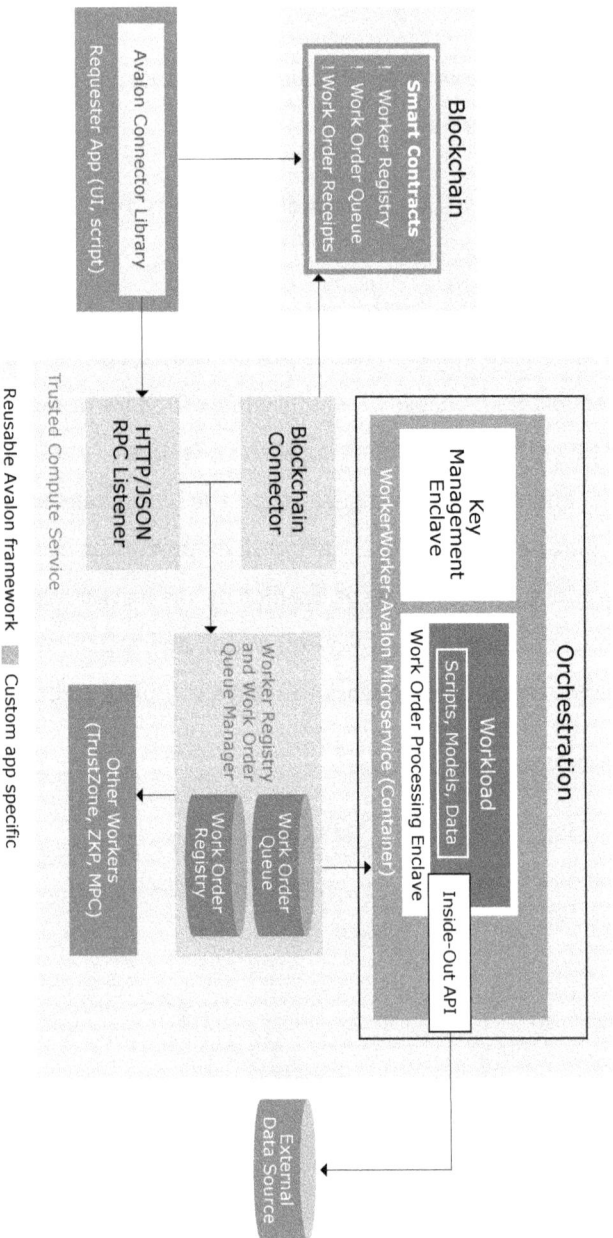

Hyperledger Avalon architecture[63]

63   "Avalon Overview." https://github.com/hyperledger/avalon/tree/main/docs.

Avalon supports and has plans for several options, including the use of trusted execution environments beyond Intel SGX, end-to-end data encryption, worker attestation, worker queues, key management, and other features. At the time of this writing, it serves as a working example of how blockchain can be combined with off-chain processing for trusted data processing, with variations of this approach likely in the future.

Other examples of secure data processing were provided in Chapter 9, including proposals from Microsoft, R3, and communities such as the Confidential Consortium Framework. These initiatives are further supported by various open-source projects from the Linux Foundation Confidential Computing Consortium including the Open Enclave SDK (https://github.com/openenclave/openenclave). Regardless of the approach, the high-level goal remains the same—establish a trusted, performant, and verifiable compute mechanism to ensure workloads execute as expected. Decentralized cloud computing, marketplaces, and use cases involving intensive data processing are all examples that can benefit from this execution model.

Finally, beyond secure data execution, blockchain may be used to manage and control analytical models. For example, it may be necessary to keep a complete audit history of not only the results of an analytical model, but also the model itself (with version), along with a representation of the related training data (via hashing). Blockchain, or alternative options such as ledger databases, can be used to store this metadata in a tamper-resistant fashion and make it available to all parties having a vested interest in this type of information. Microsoft has provided research[64] using a public blockchain for this capability, and techniques such as federated learning or swarm learning,[65] along with permissioned blockchains, have been proposed to allow organizations to train analytical models collaboratively without having to share or expose data. So, while blockchain is not the only answer to problems associated with data processing and analytics, it has the potential to provide enhanced data security, privacy, auditing, and confidentiality.

SCALING BLOCKCHAIN SOLUTIONS

Amongst factors such as availability, reliability, and security, performance is a key consideration for applications built and deployed in the enterprise. From scanning packages to running an airline or financial market, the number of batch and real-time enterprise data and process flows can be immense. Any technology deployed must be able to scale to handle not only today's data and business requirements, but also future demands. Performance has historically been a concern for enterprises looking at blockchain technology, but new solutions are emerging to address limitations. This includes improving overall transaction throughput and the amount of time it takes

---

[64] "Sharing Updatable Models (SUM) on Blockchain," GitHub documentation, https://github.com/microsoft/0xDeCA10B.

[65] Stefanie Warnat-Herresthal, Hartmut Schultze et al., "Swarm Learning for Decentralized and Confidential Clinical Machine Learning," *Nature* 594 (2021): 265–70, https://doi.org/10.1038/s41586-021-03583-3.

to finalize a transaction. These solutions go beyond simply throwing more hardware at the problem; they focus on new processing and architectural schemes.

I have already covered several options for improving blockchain performance including the role of consensus algorithms and transaction finality, alternative DLT data structures such as directed acyclic graphs, delivering data over point-to-point private channels, and off-chain capabilities to perform compute-intensive tasks or optimize storage requirements. The choices available depend both on the blockchain technology stack and whether it is consumed as a public or permissioned network, but options exist in most cases. The trick, of course, is to develop approaches that maintain appropriate levels of decentralization and security. I won't cover specific blockchain framework performance features because those are quite varied, but in recent years, generalized techniques have been introduced to address problems of blockchain scale and performance, some of which I cover next.

Sharding

Block size and its impact on performance is often discussed as one potential solution. While adding more transactions to a block can improve throughput, it will only work up to a certain point. Eventually, the amount of compute power required to run a node and validate transactions will become substantial. In public blockchains such as Ethereum, this leads to higher centralization risk because

only a small number of large organizations would be able to afford
such capacity. Alternative approaches are required.

Sharding is one such approach. With sharding, the work of building and verifying the blockchain is split across many nodes. This
is similar to what you might encounter in a database, where data is
split horizontally across many nodes such that no one node needs
to handle all data and queries. Sharding allows blockchain nodes to
process a subset of the network's transactions and manage a portion of the ledger. Each shard has its own set of validators (which
may be randomly assigned) and shares certain data elements with
a main network. Management tasks, such as assigning validators
to shards or supporting cross-shard transactions, are supported
by a main network.

Networks such as the NEAR blockchain (https://near.org/) and
Zilliqa (https://www.zilliqa.com/) have incorporated sharding into
their platforms, and Ethereum (at the time of this writing) is in
the process of rolling out the Beacon Chain (https://ethereum.org
/en/eth2/beacon-chain/) shard chain functionality. Various permissioned frameworks also include sharding as a way to achieve greater
parallelism within their environments.

Sharding, however, is not without its challenges,[66] including sin-

---

[66] "Sharding," Ethereum Foundation,
https://ethereum.org/en/upgrades/sharding/#main-content.

gle-shard takeover attacks, fraud detection, the need to coordinate cross-shard communication, and more. Related topics continue to be discussed, such as the use of sharding for transactional or computational functionality versus state sharding and shard rebalancing. Regardless, sharding offers potential for building high-performance networks.

Layer 2 Protocols

Layer 2 protocols take a different approach to performance. Instead of scaling the main blockchain network ("layer 1") and requiring complex changes to core blockchain protocols, layer 2 protocols shift the bulk of activity to an off-chain or secondary layer. Batched layer 2 transactions can be anchored to the main network, and by offloading processing to a separate layer, transaction rates, costs, and confirmation times can be improved while maintaining appropriate levels of security.

Layer 2 protocols are commonly used with public blockchain networks and are typically categorized as state channels, sidechains, or rollups. Sidechains[67] were introduced in Chapter 3, and are a secondary blockchain attached to a main network such as Ethereum. This secondary blockchain may have its own consensus and security systems, be deployed as a private or public blockchain,

---

[67] EthHub, s.v. "Sidechains,"
https://docs.ethhub.io/ethereum-roadmap/layer-2-scaling/sidechains/.

and process transactions independently from the main network. After processing is complete, the results of these transactions can be moved and stored on the main network.

State channels[68] also offload processing from the main network, but instead of having transactions available to everyone in the layer 2 network (a property of sidechains), channel transactions occur directly between the involved participants. Channels are open and closed by the participants, involving interaction with the main network, but all intermediate transactions travel directly between participants without main network involvement. This improves performance and increases privacy, but does require up-front knowledge of the participants that will be involved in the transactions.

Chapter 9 discussed zk-rollups, where individual transactions are "rolled up" into a single transaction in an off-chain environment, and a cryptographic proof is generated and submitted to the main network. Rollups[69] can be either optimistic (fraud proofs) or zero knowledge (validity proofs) to allow the network or participants to verify the batched transactions are correct. Only minimal data (the net effect of a set of transactions) is required to be stored on the main network. Rollups are relatively new and continuously evolving, but it is expected that this area will continue to grow, with

[68] "State Channels," EthHub documentation, https://docs.ethhub.io/ethereum-roadmap/layer-2-scaling/state-channels/.

[69] "Scaling," Ethereum Foundation documentation, https://ethereum.org/en/developers/docs/scaling/layer-2-rollups/.

opportunity to further improve performance by combining them with techniques such as sharding.

Layer 2 protocols are developing rapidly with many solutions being introduced, including Plasma sidechains (https://docs.ethhub.io /ethereum-roadmap/layer-2-scaling/plasma/), Lightning Network channels (http://lightning.network/), and Loopring rollups (https:// loopring.org/#/). Polygon (https://polygon.technology/) is another example of an organization building Ethereum-compatible block-chain frameworks to improve overall performance and security. Each of these has trade-offs and are relatively new and not yet widely adopted, but this work is key to future enterprise adoption and continued network growth.

Given its focus on the enterprise, one additional approach worth mentioning is the open-source Baseline Protocol (https://docs.base line-protocol.org/) and the corresponding Baseledger blockchain reference implementation. The Baseline Protocol is "an approach to using a public blockchain (for example, a mainnet) as the common frame of reference between disparate distributed systems, including traditional corporate systems of record, databases, state machines, or even different blockchains."[70] Targeted at enterprise use cases involving cross-organizational data sharing and workflows, the protocol uses pluggable layer 1 capabilities as a way to manage

---

[70] Martin Jung et al., *Baseledger: Public-Permissioned, Council Governed Network for Enterprises (Whitepaper v1.0)*, February 25, 2021, https://baseledger.net/storage/app/media/docs/Baseledger.pdf.

common frames of reference[71] and store proofs, while private enterprise data is kept off-chain in a layer 2 solution. This would allow organizations to record workflow results, such as the payment of an invoice using zk-rollups without having to expose sensitive enterprise data. Much more detail is provided in the Baseline Protocol and Baseledger (https://baseledger.net/) sites. Although in its early stages of development, the initiative offers another way to scale enterprise blockchains that looks interesting.

OTHER CHALLENGES

I could continue discussing the technical challenges impacting blockchain adoption in the enterprise, but these are not the only difficulties that must be overcome. If only it were that easy.

To deploy blockchain applications successfully, other non-technical factors must be considered, including:

- **Organizational structure and culture.** Is your organization ready to participate in decentralized, distributed business networks? Does this processing model align to your overall organizational strategy, and do you have the necessary executive-level support?

---

[71] "Glossary," Baseline Protocol documentation, https://docs.baseline-protocol.org/baseline-basics/glossary.

- **Legal, regulatory, or industry requirements.** Is a blockchain-based solution permissible within the current regulatory boundaries of your industry? Are there restrictions on how data can be handled, such as the need to conform to General Data Protection Regulation (GDPR) rules or data sovereignty requirements? How does private or confidential data need to be handled, both in terms of what can be stored on-chain and what can be shared with other participants? What audit requirements are needed by the business for legal purposes?

- **Error handling.** What is the implication of persisting an "error" (for example, bad data) to a tamper-resistant, distributed ledger? How will errors be handled? How will an error made by another participant potentially impact your business? What options do you have in such a situation?

- **Vendor lock-in.** How will you avoid being tied into one vendor's technology, which, given the pace of change in the blockchain industry, may not exist in the future? Does your team have the right skills for developing against or deploying a blockchain network? What standards (data formats, for example) may be used within your industry to facilitate switching to a different platform in the future?

- **SLA determination and KPI measurement.** How will you measure the value obtained by developing against or deploying a blockchain network? How will associated costs be predicted? What SLAs are provided by the network, and do these align with the needs of the business?

- **Network structure and governance.** Are you able to join an existing industry blockchain consortium that meets your business requirements, or is a new consortium needed? What type of blockchain network (private, permissioned, public, or hybrid) is most appropriate for your needs?

Whether creating a new network and consortium, or joining an existing network, the network structure and governance model is critically important. Blockchain networks are not only technically challenging to establish, but also complex to manage and govern, especially given the often-diverse backgrounds, maturity levels, participant goals, and "coopetition" that can exist. The creation of appropriate governance models, supported technology features, decision-making processes, funding, IP ownership, entrance/exit criteria, penalty structures, marketing activities, and legal structures all heavily influence the success of the network.

Developing strategies for each of these non-technical considerations can be more complicated and time-consuming than the technology itself! There are numerous examples of successful blockchain proof-of-concepts in the industry that did not advance further due to the complexities of establishing a network of multiple participants, concerns about non-functional requirements, legal or regulatory restrictions, or an incompatible organizational structure or culture. If the intention is to deploy this technology in production for business purposes, it is important for you to be aware of these factors and ensure each is appropriately addressed.

IS BLOCKCHAIN RIGHT FOR YOU?

Chapter 5 introduced ledger databases as one alternative to blockchain for certain use cases. Cloud-based or software-as-a-service (SaaS) applications are other options, along with simple B2B protocols. Enterprises today have learned blockchain is not the answer to everything, but it can provide value when applied to the right use case. How do you know if blockchain is right for you, or if other options are better suited to your needs?

As with any technology, the first step is to gather a list of candidate use cases. Don't worry about analyzing these in depth as to whether they are appropriate for a blockchain solution. At this point, it is only important to select use cases, processes, or workflows that could potentially benefit from a new approach. Ensure the business value behind these use cases is clear, and that you are not contemplating the use of blockchain simply because of its hype.

The next step is to evaluate and rank each use case against decision criteria, with the desired goal of selecting one or two to move forward. It may include moving to a proof-of-concept, researching and testing existing solutions, or selecting a partner for joint collaboration. The evaluation can be done, for example, by scoring with points and weights during a workshop or other form of collaboration. Regardless of your technique, it is important to have representation from various parts of the business and not just the people who want to add blockchain to their resume.

Decision Criteria

Your decision criteria should include both technical and non-technical factors. A blockchain may be technically possible, but if the current regulatory environment will not permit such a deployment, then that use case is obviously not worth prioritizing until the environment changes. The following is a list of sample questions that can be used as a starting point, but you will want to drill down on each of these to create criteria appropriate for your circumstances and organizational strategy.

- How large is the potential business network or number of participants? Minimum initial size? Possible maximum size? Would each network participant be able to access or store all information? Do transactions and data need to be partitioned across the network?

- How much data would be stored in the blockchain? What type of data would be stored? Does all data need to be stored on the ledger, or would the ledger be augmented with off-chain capabilities? Who would develop, govern, and manage the off-chain capabilities?

- What would be the performance and transaction processing requirements of the network?

- How complex is the automation or business logic that the network would be expected to support?

- What would be the required trust, integrity, and security requirements?

- How would participants access the network? How advanced are any expected data retrieval requirements?

- What legal, regulatory, or industry constraints would be placed on the network?

- What would be the level of decentralization needed? Would the network be permissioned, or is there a need to interoperate with a public network such as Ethereum?

- Do you need or plan to introduce tokenization to support the creation of digital products?

- What level of interoperability would be needed, either between the network and enterprise systems, within a single network, or between different blockchain networks?

Your responses to these types of questions should start to make it obvious whether blockchain is a fit for your use cases. For example, if tamper-resistance is identified as the only true key requirement, then a ledger database such as AWS QLDB may be sufficient, and an entire blockchain solution is not needed. If the use case only involves data coordination between parties, then a cloud-based database with an appropriate set of APIs may work instead.

If it is still unclear, then a small proof-of-concept can often sway the decision one way or the other. Regardless, if you make it past these steps, and the use case and business value still hold, then you are likely on your way to developing your solution in a blockchain context.

FINAL THOUGHTS

Blockchain is a complex topic generating plenty of passionate opinions on its use in the enterprise. Regardless of which way you are leaning, there is no doubt that blockchain and associated research into its enterprise applicability continues to evolve rapidly. While your organization may not be fully ready to dive into the technology today, it is important to be aware of its capabilities and potential areas of use.

Blockchain won't exist alone, but it just might be that one area of innovation capable of providing you with a competitive advantage. Innovation is hard, not always obvious, and can be risky—but the risk of not innovating is higher. Think big, start small, reflect on your learnings, and select your use cases carefully. You just might be surprised!

Chapter 11

THE ROLE OF
TOKENIZATION

Admittedly, this was a challenging chapter to put together given the substantial amount of tokenization, NFT, digital assets, and decentralized finance (DeFi) activity occurring in the blockchain community. It seems like there is a new approach or concept introduced *daily*. Plus, as with all chapters in this book, drilling down to the next level of detail really requires its own book (or two). It is also likely that by the time this book is released, the market will have moved to the next innovation cycle. With that as background, I decided that instead of teaching trading strategies, describing DeFi products, sharing token purchase recommendations, or providing investment advice, this chapter would cover core concepts of tokenization and its applicability to the enterprise. These concepts shouldn't change, even if the way they are technically supported or delivered does.

Tokenization, introduced in Chapter 3, currently receives a lot of attention from both the blockchain community and general media. News stories describing the sale of a piece of digital art as a non-fungible token[72] (NFT) for over $69 million have helped spread the hype, and the rapid pace of innovation and corresponding emergence of numerous startups make this an exciting area. But this is not just hype. Tokenization shows one of the most potentially revolutionary uses of blockchain in the enterprise. The promise of programmable digital assets, new business models, and novel ways of delivering goods and services through decentralized business networks has triggered the attention of numerous enterprises, with more to come.

What exactly are these tokens? How do they differ from the coins and ICOs (initial coin offerings) that were so popular in the past? Beyond art, CryptoKitties,[73] and NBA TopShot[74] "moments," how do tokens apply to the enterprise? To answer these questions, I start by describing the types of tokens in the community, and then I apply these concepts to enterprise use cases. So, if you are still with me and not working with your favorite JPEG editing tool on a creation for OpenSea (https://opensea.io/), let's begin by looking at the characteristics and types of tokens typically found in the market.

---

[72] Beeple, *Everydays: The First 5000 Days*, 2021, non-fungible token (jpg), https://onlineonly.christies.com/s/beeple-first-5000-days/beeple-b-1981-1/112924.

[73] CryptoKitties homepage, https://www.cryptokitties.co/.

[74] NBA Top Shot homepage, https://nbatopshot.com/.

TOKENS OR COINS?

To start, it's important to define the terms "token" and "coin." Each can be found in a variety of contexts, which can definitely lead to some confusion! Both are digital assets, but their roles in a blockchain can be very different. Coins—also referred to as cryptocurrencies, protocol tokens, or native tokens (the confusion starts already)—are the native asset of a blockchain network. Bitcoin (BTC), ether (ETH), and ADA are examples of such assets and integral parts of a Bitcoin, Ethereum, and Cardano blockchain network, respectively. In public blockchain networks, these coins are used for many purposes, including miner rewards, transaction spam prevention, transaction fees, and payments. Coins also support the launch of initial coin offerings (ICOs), where a crypto-token or utility token is created on a blockchain as part of a new project launch and given to investors in exchange for coins or fiat currency.

Coins are a critical component of what makes public blockchain networks work. They influence the behavior and success of the network, with much of this function derived from game theory[75] principles. When combined with cryptography, participants like miners and traders are incentivized through rewards to act honestly, or they risk losing money and being removed from the network. Blockchain's transparency, embedded rules, and equal sharing of information sets the strategies for participants, and each will

---

[75] Wikipedia, s.v. "Game theory," last modified May 12, 2022, 03:17 (UTC), https://en.wikipedia.org/wiki/Game_theory

choose the plan that maximizes their ability to earn coins. In game theory, this is known as the Nash Equilibrium.[76] Participants are competing (for mining rewards, as an example), aware of each other's strategies, and have nothing to gain by changing only their own strategy.

Conversely, tokens, also called crypto-tokens, are built on top of existing blockchain networks and leverage network functions such as smart contracts, consensus, cryptography, and the underlying tamper-resistant distributed ledger. Tokens can represent almost anything physical or digital and are often used with decentralized applications (dApps) to support end-user functions. They are programmable via smart contracts, self-describing, decentralized, and transparent. Anyone can review the underlying smart contract code to understand the logic, and it is possible to obtain the complete ownership history of a token by querying the ledger. Some tokens act as a store of value since they can be saved (for example, in a wallet) and later used, while others provide a method of exchange for goods, services, or other digital assets.

Tokens may be incorporated into private or permissioned blockchain networks, but most tokens today are built on top of public networks or included in layer 2 networks or sidechains. At the time of this writing, Ethereum is the most popular blockchain network

[76] Wikipedia, s.v. "Nash equilibrium," last modified May 21, 2022, 01:14 (UTC), https://en.wikipedia.org/wiki/Nash_equilibrium.

on which tokens are built, but other networks such as Algorand (https://www.algorand.com/) and Solana (https://solana.com/) are becoming popular.

Early tokens for Ethereum or Ethereum-compatible networks are often referred to as ERC-20 tokens because they follow one of the defined Ethereum Request for Comments (ERC) token standards.[77] ERC standards are used by developers to create smart contracts that follow a pre-defined set of rules for token implementation, ensuring all tokens of a particular type are interoperable and provide the same basic level of functionality. Other standards—such as ERC-721 (NFTs), ERC-1400 (security tokens), and ERC-1155 (one contract for multiple token types)—have since been defined, allowing developers to create tokens that best meet their requirements.

Coins and tokens are synergistic, and the value of each can be inter-dependent. Greater demand for a token can increase the demand for the underlying native coin, thereby increasing its value. Tokens also require the use of coins to perform certain functions, such as creating or "minting" a token and saving changes to the underlying ledger, which can also impact the value of the underlying coin. This dependency, however, has created concerns for networks like Ethereum. Performance challenges and high transaction costs have driven the creation of competing networks that promise larger

---

[77] "ERC Token Standards," EthHub documentation, https://docs.ethhub.io/built-on-ethereum/erc-token-standards/what-are-erc-tokens/.

transaction volumes, faster block finality times, and lower costs. However, regardless of the network on which they are based, tokens offer great flexibility and can serve many purposes.

Types of Tokens

As mentioned, tokens can represent almost anything digital or physical, plus provide the holder with the right to perform an action either inside or outside the blockchain network. I provide specific examples later in this chapter, but despite the broad range of possibilities, tokens are typically grouped into categories similar to those below. And don't worry! I'm sure you will immediately note the absence of the popular fungible and non-fungible (NFT) tokens. I cover these in a separate section of this chapter.

- **Security (Asset) tokens.** Security tokens[78] provide holders with complete or fractional ownership in an asset that has value, such as shares in a company or real estate. Unlike utility tokens, security tokens are subject to legal guidelines based on identity, jurisdiction, or asset category, and act similarly to bonds or shares in a publicly traded company. Security tokens eliminate the need for traditional paper and are completely digitized on a blockchain. Polymath (https://polymath.network/) is an example of a network designed to support security tokens, and countries like

---

[78] Security Token Standard homepage, https://thesecuritytokenstandard.org/.

Switzerland have published guidelines[79] on how current financial regulations apply to these tokens. Holders of security tokens are typically expecting to make a profit, so these tokens are often treated as regular securities from a regulatory standpoint.

- **Governance tokens.** Governance tokens are used to provide holders with a vote on the operations of the network itself. These tokens are often associated with decentralized autonomous organizations (DAOs) that guide the direction of the protocol, develop project roadmaps, or decide on new features. Voting by token holders is typically executed on-chain, with approved changes automatically controlled via smart contracts or performed manually by the team supporting the project. Maker (MKR) is one example of a governance token (at the time of this writing), allowing holders to influence the direction of the DAI stablecoin via the Maker Protocol (https://makerdao.com /en/governance).

- **Utility (application) tokens.** Utility tokens provide a holder with access to the goods and services a project will deliver. These are one of the most common types of tokens in the blockchain community because they allow holders

---

[79] Rick Delafont, "Swiss Financial Regulators Publish ICO Guidelines," *NewsBTC*, 2018, https://www.newsbtc.com/news/ico/ swiss-financial-regulators-publish-pretty-reasonable-ico-guidelines/.

to access the capabilities or functions provided by the issuing project. Utility tokens are designed to be used within the blockchain system from which they are issued and, unlike security tokens, are not designed as investments. Filecoin (FIL), Civic (CVC), and Chainlink (LINK) are examples of utility tokens, with each project using them for access and incentives.

- **Payment tokens.** Payment tokens are general purpose stores of value used to pay for goods and services. Bitcoin, for example, can be considered a payment token because it can be used to pay for specific goods or services. However, payment tokens are not widely used, given the degree of price fluctuation and value change that can occur in a short period of time, especially compared to fiat currency. Businesses accepting this form of payment take a risk because the value can drop suddenly. Payment tokens are likely to be replaced by stablecoins, a class of cryptocurrency designed to fluctuate less.

- **Data tokens.** Data tokens are used to represent a particular data element, or to provide the right to access or process data. Introduced in response to the growing interest in data marketplaces and data sharing between organizations, data tokens allow holders to access and process data provided by another organization or entity.

Although commonly used as financial instruments, tokens are actually much more. They can represent physical assets (wine, diamonds, real estate), digital assets (art, music), securities, voting privileges, application functions, enterprise assets (invoices, bills of lading, data), and likely numerous other assets that have yet to be tokenized. Regardless of their use, remember that tokens are not just a digital representation of an asset; they are programmable via smart contracts, self-describing, and encapsulate the rules of whatever it is they represent. This is very different from what we have today, where the rules governing the behavior of assets as we know them are typically on paper, not directly bound to the asset itself, and the history of the asset is not tracked throughout its lifetime in an agreed-upon, tamper-resistant, and transparent manner. These characteristics are what make tokens so interesting to the enterprise and represent a great opportunity for the future of digital initiatives.

Of course, as with any new technology, legal and regulatory constructs have yet to catch up. Ownership rights, copyright considerations, Know Your Customer (KYC) and Anti-Money Laundering (AML) requirements, privacy concerns, data sovereignty requirements, and many other regulatory frameworks have yet to adapt to this new digital paradigm. Therefore, before beginning any tokenization project, be sure to identify these risks as part of your research; certain use cases may not yet be possible in current regulatory environments.

Fungible Tokens

Before diving into non-fungible tokens, I want to touch on fungible tokens, so you are aware of the characteristics of both. Fungible tokens are derived from the economic concept of fungibility[80] and represent goods or assets that are indistinguishable from each other. They are divisible and non-unique, can be uniformly accepted and interchanged, and act as a store of value. Bitcoin is one example of a fungible token. One Bitcoin can be divided into smaller units, interchanged with another as their value is equal (disregarding transfer times), and each Bitcoin is standardized and treated identically across the entire Bitcoin network. These properties make fungible tokens similar to commodity money or assets such as USD, gold, or silver. In Ethereum, and other Ethereum-compatible networks, fungible tokens use the ERC-20 standard to ensure interoperability via a common structure.

Non-fungible Tokens (NFTs)

Non-fungible tokens may receive most of their media attention from art and tweet sales,[81] but NFTs have much broader applicability in the blockchain world. NFTs are obviously tokens and can

---

[80] Jake Frankenfield, "Fungibility," Investopedia, updated May 7, 2022, https://www.investopedia.com/terms/f/fungibility.asp.

[81] Taylor Locke, "Jack Dorsey Sells His First Tweet Ever As An NFT for over $2.9 Million," *CNBC*, March 22, 2021, https://www.cnbc.com/2021/03/22/jack-dorsey-sells-his-first-tweet-ever-as-an-nft-for-over-2point9-million.html.

represent physical or digital assets. However, the key element that differentiates NFTs from other token types is that they represent unique programmable assets on a blockchain. They are indivisible, irreplaceable, traceable, and verifiable. Ownership of a token may be transferred, or an NFT may be traded for another NFT, but they are not interchangeable because the value associated with each token is different.

That's a lot of information in a single paragraph! But the uniqueness property, combined with the features and programmability of the underlying blockchain network used by the NFT, are what makes NFTs interesting for representing a wide range of assets. NFTs can even inject scarcity into the system because the supply is controlled. NFT creators can decide to create only one copy or several replicas, such as tickets to a sporting event. Whether one or one thousand NFTs are created, each would have a unique identifier and a publicly verifiable owner. This controlled scarcity assists in defining the supply, demand, and corresponding value of the NFT; certain markets place a high value on the ownership of an original, much like original paintings are typically worth more than copies.

Given the need to bundle additional data elements into the token, such as asset metadata and ownership details, NFTs currently use the ERC-721 standard instead of ERC-20. This makes different NFTs compatible with each other and, assuming appropriate functionality has been built into the token smart contracts, allows them to be traded on the same network.

NFT Challenges

Tokenizing a digital or physical asset as an NFT is not, however, without its challenges:

- **Asset linking.** Whether NFTs represent physical or digital assets, the need to verify the linked asset is important. For example, if the NFT represents digital art, where is the art stored? Is it stored on the blockchain along with the NFT (rare, given the cost of doing so)? Or is it stored on a different blockchain, in a decentralized storage system such as IPFS, or on a private server? What is the risk of this "link" becoming invalid due to a loss of access to the server, or if IPFS nodes no longer host the data? For physical assets, these risks are greater because it can be difficult to verify that the asset exists, in the state promised, and that it stays as described over its lifetime. IoT, tamper-proof packaging, and cryptographic anchors[82] can help with linking, but the risks must be assessed and appropriate off-chain processes assigned to manage them.

- **Ownership.** As mentioned, the degree of ownership of an underlying NFT asset is not always perfectly clear. A purchaser, for example, cannot assume the NFT creator had the underlying rights to tie the asset to the token in the

---

[82] Simple English Wikipedia, s.v. "Cryptographic anchor," last modified June 1, 2021, 11:55 (UTC), https://simple.wikipedia.org/wiki/Cryptographic_anchor.

first place, and NFT ownership does not necessarily mean you have the associated copyright.[83] This implies that the original owner may still have the right to reproduce or create derivate works based on the copyrighted work, potentially destroying the value of the token. This area of law can be quite complex and varies across jurisdictions, so be certain to research any underlying legal and regulatory implications of the tokenized assets being developed or acquired, or you risk an unpleasant surprise.

- **Security and fraud.** Given lagging regulations and lack of oversight mechanisms, concerns about token fraud and security remain high. For example, it has been shown that the lack of KYC and AML guidelines makes it possible to launder money with NFTs. Data must be carefully shared across the blockchain network to maintain privacy requirements, and key management remains an important consideration because a lost or compromised private key can render a tokenized asset inaccessible. Hacking and other fraudulent activities, such as altering the underlying physical asset as noted previously, are also important factors to consider. Therefore, it is important to put plans in place to recover from these actions should such an event occur, and to support NFT transactions with traditional paper when needed.

---

[83] Exclusive rights in copyrighted works, 17 U.S.C. section 106, Cornell Law School, Legal Information Institute, https://www.law.cornell.edu/uscode/text/17/106.

I hope I've clarified the use of coins and tokens in the blockchain community. Remember, tokens, and especially NFTs, are not just about the digitization of an asset. They are also an opportunity for enterprises to create new digital products, build communities around a brand or service, and hopefully drive additional revenue and value. Projects such as the NBA's TopShot have shown the effectiveness of NFTs for improving customer engagement, clarifying customer segments, and providing token holders with platinum features not available to people outside of the NFT community. So, should you be looking at tokenization? What are some additional enterprise examples? Good questions! I cover these topics next.

NFTS AND ENTERPRISE USE CASES

Why Tokenize?

As described, NFTs are unique, programmable assets on a blockchain with verifiable ownership and value influenced through controlled scarcity. These properties make NFTs extremely flexible, applicable to numerous enterprise use cases, and capable of providing organizations with a variety of benefits, including:

- **Verifiable ownership.** Given that NFTs are based on an underlying blockchain platform, ownership information and transfers are transparently recorded and tamper-resistant. The entire ownership history may be verified, and attributes such as the original creator can be associated with the token throughout its lifecycle. However, legal and regulatory considerations need to be considered to ensure the end result of acquiring a token is as expected. There are also questions surrounding the uniqueness of tokens and level of interoperability between different blockchain networks.

- **"Always on" global accessibility.** The functionality provided by NFTs is accessible from anywhere in the world, at any time, by anyone. Sophisticated hardware or software is not needed; a simple web application or smartphone is sufficient, although this access can still be a challenge in some parts of the world.

- **Self-describing and programmable.** NFTs embed all of the metadata and logic needed to function via smart contracts. Defined logic is programmable, transparent, and verifiable, with new business models expressed as code. However, complex code can still result in bugs and expose opportunities for hacking.

- **Decentralized with no middleman.** Using blockchain as the basis for NFTs reduces the need for a central third party. This potentially lowers costs, reduces processing times, and increases security because there is no central party or application to attack. As discussed in Chapter 4, however, some degree of centralization will still exist as complete decentralization is not currently possible in blockchain networks.

- **Flexible finance.** Information associated with NFTs is transparent and equally available to all parties participating in a transaction, which aids in removing unfair advantages for one participant. NFTs can simplify the processes involved with shared or fractionalized asset ownership, and their programmability enables them to be used as collateral for loans, as mechanisms for collecting royalties, and for numerous other financial arrangements. NFTs may also improve liquidity and portfolio diversification because fractionalization of an asset broadens the pool of people able to participate in its ownership. Expensive equipment, intellectual property, and real estate are examples that may benefit from fractional ownership structures and NFTs.

Of course, the benefits recognized depend on the specific scenarios and use cases implemented as part of a tokenization strategy. Risks exist, but so do opportunities for almost any vertical. Further examples are listed below, but this list is not exhaustive. Use cases and token-based applications are constantly evolving as startups and enterprise companies test the possibilities of the technology.

Art, Music, and Collectibles	Sports and Entertainment
Gaming	Customer Engagement
Digital Twins	Supply Chain Management
Decentralized Finance	Real Estate
Intellectual Property	Identity
Loyalty Programs	Electricity
Carbon Credits	Tickets
Bills of Lading / Invoices	Loan Collateral

The potential impact of NFTs in the enterprise is substantial. NFTs represent much more than a digital or physical asset. In some cases, they can make you part of a community or brand or represent financial and portfolio diversification opportunities. It is also possible that in the future NFTs will enable the microtransactions necessary for autonomous IoT devices to use each other for services. I'm definitely looking forward to watching this area evolve in the months and years to come.

DECENTRALIZED FINANCE (DEFI)

Before closing out this chapter, I wanted to briefly discuss decentralized finance because there is a huge amount of effort currently being spent in this area. Similar to the aforementioned properties of NFTs, DeFi brings programmable financial products and services to the decentralized world, and thus to any user with an internet connection and cryptocurrency wallet. By decomposing traditional, centralized, and monolithic financial applications into smaller, reusable, and composable financial functions, DeFi provides potential advantages. These include the reduction or elimination of intermediaries, reduced fees, embedded programmability, increased transparency, and broad accessibility.

DeFi expands beyond cryptocurrencies and payments and attempts to provide a global, open alternative to almost every financial service or product in use today. From simple loans to complex financial instruments, the building blocks or dApps that comprise the DeFi market are easily composable, enabling new products to be created quickly. As with NFTs, smart contracts make much of this capability possible. The logic behind DeFi products is transparent and open, and all transactions are recorded against public blockchain networks such as Ethereum and Solana. Combinations of DeFi and traditional financial products are also possible, providing enterprises with the opportunity to combine these emerging capabilities with existing systems.

Smart contracts and an underlying public blockchain network are not the only elements used in DeFi solutions. For example, a typical DeFi component stack may involve the architectural layers highlighted in the diagram below:

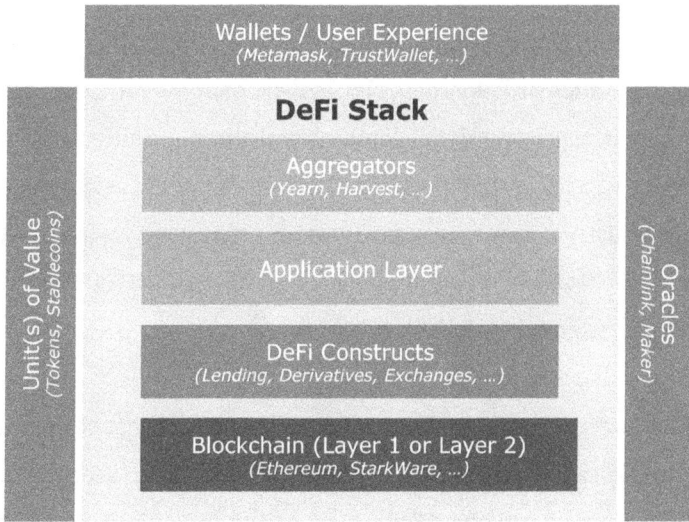

Sample DeFi component stack

Stablecoins form the basis of many DeFi functions, and are used with the underlying blockchain native protocol token. These programmable digital currencies are designed to lower volatility in the network (compared to cryptocurrencies like BTC or ETH) and provide a reliable unit of value. This stabilization of asset value is achieved by backing or pegging the stablecoin to fiat currency (USD), to other commodities (gold) or cryptocurrencies, or to the output of an algorithm that manages value by adjusting token supply and demand. Tether, DAI, USD Coin, PAX Gold, and Ampleforth are examples of stablecoins in the market at this time. Stablecoins are also an alternative to central bank digital currencies (CBDCs) issued by banks.

Other layers of the component stack include the underlying block-chain network, layer 2 implementations, core DeFi functional building blocks such as loans, deposits, and exchanges, the application layer itself, aggregators that combine and automate different DeFi functions across exchanges, and wallets that provide the user experience. Lastly, oracles such as Chainlink play a key role in DeFi networks because they provide trusted off-chain data to smart contracts running in the network.

Similar to NFTs, DeFi has the potential to drastically change the way financial products and services are made available to users. Many people across the globe do not have access to banks or financial services, and DeFi is one possible solution to this problem. However, like NFTs, there are legal and regulatory hurdles to cross before these capabilities are broadly accepted. The DeFi world is still immature and unregulated, concerns remain regarding network performance and underlying transaction costs, and short-term solution fragmentation will continue as new projects and alternative blockchain networks emerge. Hacking[84] is also an issue, along with smart contract bugs, fraud, scam projects, and thefts or "rug pulls" (when creators abandon a project and disappear with related funds). Regardless, DeFi is an area worth watching.

---

[84] Jamie Crawley, "DeFi Has Accounted for Over 75% of Crypto Hacks in 2021," *CoinDesk*, August 10, 2021, updated September 14, 2021, https://www.coindesk.com /markets/2021/08/10/defi-has-accounted-for-over-75-of-crypto-hacks-in-2021/.

FINAL THOUGHTS

The pace of innovation and creativity in tokenization and DeFi is extremely rapid, with new ideas, startups, and digital products emerging regularly. As with any new technology focused on privacy, ownership, and financial systems, early adoption can be risky. However, governments and banks have started to take notice, with many traditional institutions exploring related use cases,[85] and regulators providing guidance.[86]

Not all attention is positive. At the time of this writing, countries such as China and India have either banned or are looking to ban cryptocurrencies outside of their own official digital currency. This raises questions about the intent of these bans, and whether considerations such as digital surveillance, government oversight, and taxes are influencing these decisions.

Regardless, representing assets as programmable, decentralized, secure, transparent, and verifiable digital products has fantastic opportunities for the enterprise. It also opens the door to new

---

[85] Tanzeel Akhtar, "About 80% of Central Banks Are Exploring CBDC Use Cases, Bison Trails Report Says," *CoinDesk*, May 19, 2021, updated September 14, 2021, https://www.coindesk.com/markets/2021/05/19/about-80-of-central-banks-are -exploring-cbdc-use-cases-bison-trails-report-says/.

[86] Nikhilesh De, "US Federal Regulator Says Banks Can Conduct Payments Using Stablecoins," *CoinDesk*, January 4, 2021, updated September 14, 2021, https://www.coindesk.com/policy/2021/01/04/us-federal-regulator-says-banks -can-conduct-payments-using-stablecoins/.

technologies (the fun stuff) such as Web3 and metaverse applications. On to the next and final chapter!

Chapter 12

LOOKING TO THE FUTURE

Blockchain has an exciting future. Whether it continues along its current trajectory, transforms into something new, or assumes a complementary role within other technology, its decentralization, privacy, security, open networks, value exchange, programmability, and community focus spark important questions:

- What is the right level of centralization (if any) for finance, banking, and asset ownership?

- How can an individual's privacy be preserved in our highly connected world?

- Will large, centralized organizations continue to be the driving force behind the internet?

- How can equal, decentralized, and integrated opportunities between individuals and organizations be achieved while meeting regulatory requirements?

- How will these requirements evolve?

- And what role will an enterprise take in any of this?

Time will tell, but disruptions to current business models across the internet are already underway, and I expect innovation related to all the topics covered in this book and others to continue at a rapid pace.

So, to close out this book, I wanted to touch on a few forward-looking blockchain-related conversations. While it is likely that some of the concepts being discussed may take years to realize if they progress at all, the potential for them to drive change in the enterprise market is substantial. It is critical for organizations to follow these conversations and look for opportunities to adopt new capabilities or risk being left behind.

FUTURE CONSIDERATIONS FOR ENTERPRISE ARCHITECTURES

Blockchain and Analytics

As previously mentioned, AI/ML currently receives a large amount of attention in the market, with most enterprises incorporating analytics capabilities into their overall data strategy. Data is extremely valuable, and the ability to derive greater insights from it is a competitive advantage. But AI/ML also has a role in blockchain, typically contributing in two areas. The first is the use of blockchain to support enterprise analytics solutions, and the second is to use AI/ML to build smarter blockchain networks.

Blockchain in enterprise architectures was covered in Chapter 10, including its role in data collection, data integrity, privacy and security, data processing, and analytical model usage. Federated and swarm learning were discussed, where blockchain becomes the mechanism by which metadata and other control data are shared across a network of nodes collaborating on executing private analytical workloads. And, the use of blockchain in open data markets was mentioned as a way to securely connect data providers with data consumers. Organizations such as OpenMined (https://www.openmined.org/), Streamr (https://streamr.network/), Numerai (https://numer.ai/), and the Ocean Protocol (https://oceanprotocol.com/) are some that serve these markets, with tokenization incorporated to support exchanges of value, rewards, and incentives.

However, AI/ML also can extend blockchain frameworks. AI-powered oracles, AI-focused consensus algorithms such as Proof of Learning,[87] and AI embedded in DeFi platforms are all opportunities enabled by the convergence of AI/ML and blockchain. Expanded decentralized autonomous organization (DAO) capabilities, enhanced transaction security, deeper ledger data analysis, and smarter smart contracts are also possibilities. Blockchains generate terabytes of data each day and contain large amounts of metadata in the form of smart contracts, which are also a proverbial gold mine for analytics. Challenges exist, such as the need for determinism across the network (so nodes executing AI/ML models must agree on the results) and the ability to explain "why AI did what it did" to users and regulatory bodies, but the intersection of AI/ML and blockchain introduces many opportunities for innovation.

Blockchain and Integration

Similar to AI/ML, blockchain and integration typically meet in two contexts. The first, covered in Chapter 10, includes blockchain in an overall enterprise IT stack that facilitates its integration with enterprise applications and streamlines the movement of data using both real-time and batch mechanisms.

---

[87] Felipe Bravo-Marquez et al., "Proof-of-Learning: a Blockchain Consensus Mechanism based on Machine Learning Competitions," 2019 IEEE International Conference on Decentralized Applications and Infrastructures (DAPPCON), (Newark CA, April 2019), https://felipebravom.com/publications/dappcon2019.pdf.

The second context involves integration between blockchain networks. As I wrote, it is very likely the market will produce multiple blockchain platforms, expanding the need to share and transfer data, assets, identity, and other information seamlessly. This is true whether the networks are private or public, and in many cases, integration will need to connect networks of different types, leading to hybrid blockchain application deployments. Hyperledger Cactus (https://www.hyperledger.org/use/cactus) and Accenture's interoperability approach (https://www.accenture.com/us-en /insights/blockchain/integration-ecosystems) are projects focused on blockchain integration via specialized plugins or nodes, with other organizations such as Polygon (https://polygon.technology/), Cosmos (https://cosmos.network/), and Polkadot (https://polkadot .network/) introducing interoperability capabilities ("blockchains of blockchains") based on their networks.

DLT heterogeneity, complex multi-party coordination, limited standards, feature differences, and the need to maintain the core properties of a blockchain network during the transfer of assets and value all make the problem of blockchain network integration extremely complex. However, solving this problem will become important as the number of blockchain networks increases, and as individual participation in constructs such as Web3 and the metaverse grows.

One related item is the possible use of blockchain to support serverless computing. Common in today's cloud environments, serverless computing allows services and applications to be built and deployed without concern for the underlying hardware, virtual machines, or even containers. Only the compute resources needed to support distributed application volumes are consumed, and organizations only pay for what they use.

Today, these proprietary serverless compute environments are provided by organizations such as Amazon, Google, and Microsoft, but in the future, blockchain may expand these capabilities beyond these cloud platforms. Blockchain's smart contracts, decentralized architecture, and distributed ledger can be used to support multi-cloud serverless compute and storage environments, prevent vendor lock-in, and further lower costs by charging per instruction. Performance constraints and a lack of support for auto-scaling (both up and out) are a few current blockchain limitations that would need to be addressed, but opportunity exists for blockchain to advance current enterprise compute environments.

Blockchain and Quantum Computing

Often discussed in the context of blockchain is quantum computing and its potential impact on blockchain privacy, confidentiality, and security. Beyond the obvious advancements in compute power, which will impact functions such as blockchain mining, the concern is that advancements in quantum computing will make it possible for future applications to "break" current encryption and cryptographic algorithms. This security breach would render blockchain's public key infrastructure (PKI) useless. However, it will likely be many years before quantum computers become powerful and capable enough to break current encryption algorithms, and work has already begun on creating post-quantum encryption technologies. Strategies for incorporating these, such as soft forks, will need to be developed, and organizations will need to address not only blockchain-based applications, but any service or application (including the internet) using PKI. So, while this is not a small problem, it is a *known* problem. The bigger challenge will likely be the speed at which organizations can deploy needed changes throughout their application landscape.

Tokenization and Financial Transformation

I covered tokenization in depth in Chapter 11 and introduced many of the questions that remain for the future of coins, tokens, NFTs, and DeFi. Governance models, legal constraints, and regulatory considerations will be key areas in the upcoming months as governments attempt to tackle programmable assets, digital property, DAOs, crypto-taxes, stablecoins, central bank digital currencies (CBDCs), and the further blending of the digital and physical worlds.

Autonomous IoT devices, micropayments, new definitions of scarcity, interoperability requirements, standards development, and the potential for organizations such as Apple and Amazon to create or support their own tokens are also areas to monitor and track.

Programmable assets and the formation of communities based on these assets are huge opportunities for the enterprise, and also key drivers behind emerging metaverse and Web3 concepts.

It is also important to recognize that this shift towards tokenization and cryptocurrency is already in motion and expected to accelerate. NFTs and DeFi have exploded, with millions of dollars in equivalent fiat value regularly changing hands. Cryptocurrency adoption is increasing, with large numbers of individuals holding it in their investment portfolios. Companies such as MicroStrategy[88] hold Bitcoin on their balance sheets, and both Visa[89] and Mastercard[90] have publicly stated that cryptocurrency, CBDCs, NFTs, and stable-coins are key elements of their future business strategy. Cities such as Miami have introduced their own cryptocurrency ("MiamiCoin"), various central banks have announced plans to launch a CBDC in the upcoming years, and countries such as El Salvador[91] have adopted Bitcoin as legal tender to improve an individual's access to financial services. All of these actions point to a trend that is simply

---

[88] Sheldon Reback, "MicroStrategy Buys Another $94.2M of Bitcoin," *CoinDesk*, December 31, 2021, https://www.coindesk.com/business/2021/12/30/microstrategy -buys-another-942-million-of-bitcoin/.

[89] Julia Arvelaiz, "Visa's Fascination With Crypto: Sees 'The Future of Money,'" *Bitcoinist*, https://bitcoinist.com/visas-fascination-with-crypto-sees-the-future/.

[90] Frank Chaparro, "Mastercard EVP Jess Turner on Becoming a 'Crypto First' Company," *The Block*, November 19, 2021, https://www.theblockcrypto.com/post /124710/mastercard-evp-jess-turner-on-becoming-a-crypto-first-company.

[91] Arjun Kharpal, "El Salvador Becomes First Country to Adopt Bitcoin As Legal Tender after Passing Law," *CNBC*, June 9, 2021, https://www.cnbc.com/2021/06/09 /el-salvador-proposes-law-to-make-bitcoin-legal-tender.html.

not going away and will likely continue to build. Organizations need to look for opportunities to not only participate but also offer or embed tokenization capabilities into their own applications as customer adoption of these digital products grows.

THE WORLD BEYOND WEB 2.0

Web3

If you ask three people their definition of Web3 (or Web 3.0 as it is sometimes called, although this is not to be confused with the Semantic Web, which is also referred to as Web 3.0), you will likely receive three different answers. To some, it involves a complete reworking of the internet with blockchain technologies; to others, Web3 is simply marketing hype without any substance. Quite a range of opinions! So, what is the right answer?

Like many technologies early in their lifecycles, the answer is likely somewhere in the middle. To explain further, it helps to briefly define the precursors to Web3, namely Web 1.0 and Web 2.0.

Web 1.0 includes the early stages of the internet, where most content consisted of static web pages created by companies. This lasted for a number of years until the emergence of Web 2.0, where content became much more dynamic and generated by both individuals and organizations. This is where we sit today, with companies like Facebook, Google, Netflix, YouTube, and a few others dominating the landscape. These organizations collect and monetize the vast amounts of data associated with an individual's online activity, and they are also largely responsible for functions such as content monitoring (which sometimes involves censorship) and confidentiality.

This dominance of the internet by a few large, centralized organizations is the primary target of Web3. To some, Web3 is an opportunity to rethink the mechanics behind the internet and transition to an environment that is more open, decentralized, secure, and shared by all. Blockchain, DAOs, dApps, tokenization, smart contracts, and blockchain-based services form the basis of this new web, leading to an internet where individuals retain ownership of their data, power is no longer concentrated in a few organizations, security and privacy are enhanced, and the value of any generated content and data can be realized by all parties.

DeFi is seen as the first move towards such a world, as it enables the creation of financial products via open protocols that are programmable, composable, and accessible by anyone with an internet connection. With Web3, current internet services and companies would be replaced by new blockchain-native services, and organizations such as the Web3 Foundation (https://web3.foundation/) would support the development of new Web3 technologies via grants and other projects to produce a technology stack like the following:

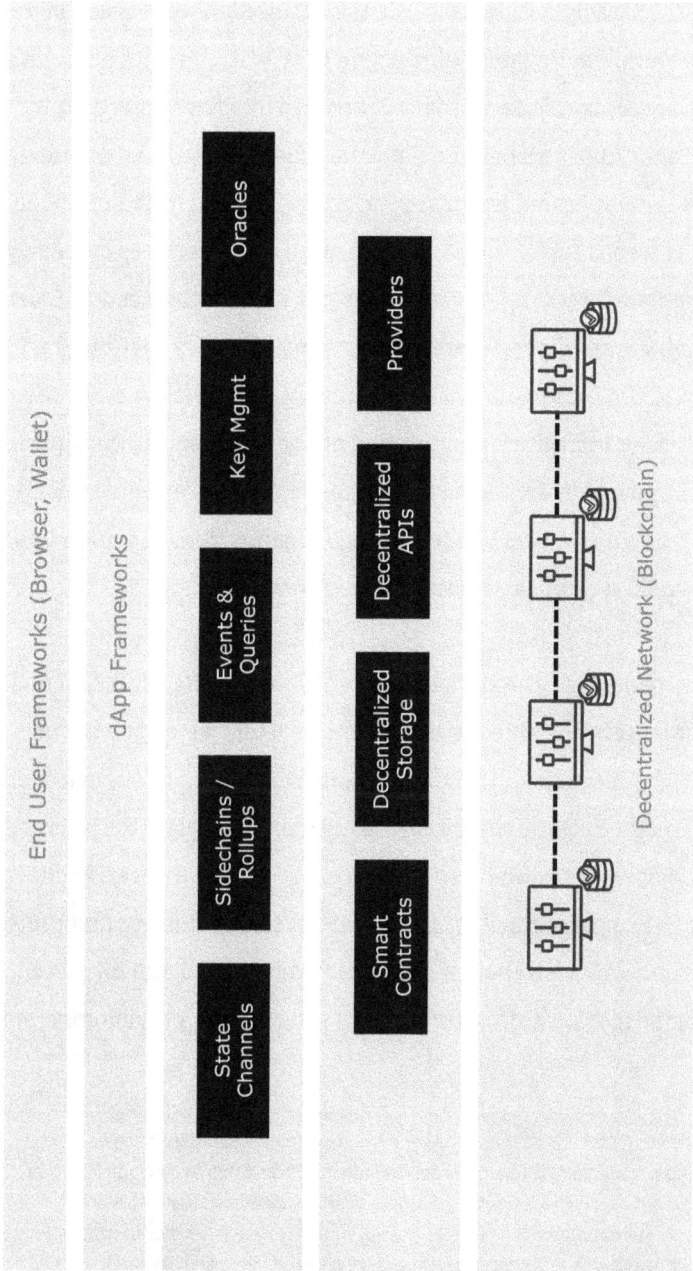

Simplified Web3 technology stack

End User Frameworks (Browser, Wallet)

dApp Frameworks

State Channels | Sidechains / Rollups | Events & Queries | Key Mgmt | Oracles

Smart Contracts | Decentralized Storage | Decentralized APIs | Providers

Decentralized Network (Blockchain)

Will this paradigm shift occur? Critics of this ambitious vision point out several challenges. Some argue that Web3, and its emerging software companies, are largely controlled by a few venture capitalists[92] and thus is no better than what exists today. The technology stack is complicated (compare the above diagram to the relatively simple web stack of Web 1.0 or 2.0), with many services currently unregulated. Moving to Web3 does not change the need to trust a small group of people or organizations (the ones that build and operate the Web3 services), and moving people away from their YouTube or Instagram accounts will not be easy. Regulatory requirements, government actions, and the presence of extremely large, well-known, and well-funded Web 2.0 organizations (Google, Meta/Facebook, etc.) will also impact this transition.

So, as mentioned, the answer lies somewhere in the middle. In reality, at least in the short to midterm, it is likely we will continue to see Web3 services and applications layered on top of current Web 2.0 structures. Quite simply, we are not going to replace the internet, its services, or the web browser anytime soon! However, I believe that DeFi, programmable assets, self-sovereign identity, and other concepts will push the boundaries of Web 2.0, and individuals will continue to transition to those Web3 services that provide concrete

---

[92] Cheyenne Ligon, "Jack Dorsey Goes on Unfollowing Frenzy After Web3 Beef," *CoinDesk*, December 22, 2021, updated December 23, 2021, https://www.coindesk.com /business/2021/12/23/jack-dorsey-goes-on-unfollowing-frenzy-after-web-3-beef/ is a current example, but the Bitcoin purists will state that other blockchain network approaches sacrifice decentralization and security for the sake of features.

value. The current "wild west" of Web3 will be eventually replaced by proven, but innovative, business models—and new opportunities for both enterprises and individuals will emerge that truly provide fair and equitable value. Will we reach the ultimate end state? The degree to which this shift occurs will be very interesting to track in the months ahead.

BLOCKCHAIN FOR DIGITAL APPLICATIONS

Metaverse Apps

Originally introduced by Neal Stephenson in his 1992 science-fiction novel *Snow Crash*, the metaverse describes a virtual world where people interact and engage with each other via digital avatars. This concept is not new. Online games, without referring to their environments as the "metaverse," have supported this form of engagement for quite some time. However, online games are siloed, closed, and centralized, which are the characteristics being altered in the metaverse's expanding definition.

Today's definition typically refers to a series of open, interconnected virtual worlds (collectively called the "metaverse") where people can interact freely and engage outside the control of a single organization. Governance is achieved through DAO structures, an individual's identity may be carried across digital environments, and commerce is supported through the use of tokens and other programmable assets. Under this definition, people can perform many of the actions that currently exist in the physical world. Assets like land and buildings, although virtual, can be bought and sold. Services can be provided, and complete economies can be formed. The user experience can vary—from current Web 2.0 two-dimensional content to immersive, augmented virtual reality—all executed in real-time. It is even possible for people to earn a living through GameFi (a combination of gaming and DeFi) and PlayToEarn experiences, where cryptocurrencies are earned by playing a game. The end result of this metaverse is game-like, but much broader than what is seen today because it is meant to be open, available to everyone, interoperable, and decentralized.

To realize this vision, blockchain is seen as one possible solution, although its use is not mandatory for realizing many attributes of the metaverse. Blockchain's many characteristics—decentralization, programmable assets, smart contracts, tamper-resistant storage, and others—offer possibilities for enabling the metaverse. And, as with Web 2.0, the core foundation underpinning the metaverse is the internet, with optional Web3 extensions.

This is a very grand vision, with many elements required before it can be realized. A lack of interoperability, standardization, governance, and digital identity make the metaverse years away from full realization. But as people move towards deeper online interactions and engagement, as communities focused on transitioning ownership and power back to the individual grow, and as innovation proceeds, the current functional gaps will narrow.

For the enterprise, it will be important to stay abreast of these trends, separate fact from fiction, and think "outside of the box" when evaluating opportunities. The enterprise of tomorrow can establish a presence in these virtual worlds, offer valuable services and assets, and further support and participate in the development of open communities and rich customer experiences. It is also possible for enterprises to adopt a subset of the metaverse to build their own "worlds" using key elements of their business. Digital twin-enabled factory floors, immersive augmented reality-enabled collaboration environments, IoT-powered healthcare, and virtual supply chains are all use case examples that might benefit from a metaverse vision.

FINAL THOUGHTS

To me, blockchain is an exciting and rapidly evolving area of technology offering substantial potential for both the enterprise and the individual. Society's current focus on supply chains, healthcare, ESG[93] considerations, identity, privacy, the circular economy, ethical analytics, community formation, open platforms, and other matters are extremely important—and blockchain, including its many tangents, has the capability to contribute positively to each one.

Already, in a very short period, blockchain has moved from its first-ever Bitcoin transaction in 2009, to broad networks of

---

[93] Environmental, Social, and Governance

blockchain-based dApps enabling global programmable assets. Private, permissioned, and public solutions have been deployed, and visions of a more inclusive, decentralized, and open technology platform available to all are resulting in rapid innovation, both in technology and in how future products and services will be delivered.

Blockchain cannot exist alone, especially in the enterprise, which I covered in detail in Chapter 10. It also has several shortcomings needing to be addressed before it can truly be seen as the core platform behind the next generation of the internet, or even the next payment system. But looking back to Chapter 1—as the world increasingly shifts to highly connected interactions, decentralized business networks, advanced technology platforms, and improved collaboration—change is needed. And while blockchain is not the only answer to this need, it certainly can play a role.

When I first sat down to write this book, my goal was to provide an easy-to-follow resource and "one-stop-shop" for readers who do not regularly live in the world of blockchain. It is my hope that this book has served as a useful guide and provided clarity on topics that can be challenging to distill into something straightforward and practical. I also hope blockchain's relevance to the enterprise is apparent; it is not just for creating the next cryptocurrency millionaire. Happy BUIDLing![94]

---

[94] An intentional misspelling of "build," much like "HODL" is a misspelling of "hold." Blockchain slang!

THIRD PARTY COPYRIGHT NOTICES

Copyright Notice for Image 15 titled "Components of a verified credential," Image 17 titled "Simple DID example," and Image 18 titled "Simple DID document":

This document includes material copied from or derived from Verifiable Credentials Data Model v1.1 (https://www.w3.org/TR/2022/REC-vc-data -model-20220303/) and Decentralized Identifiers (DIDs) v1.0 (https://www .w3.org/TR/2021/PR-did-core-20210803/). Copyright 2021 World Wide Web Consortium, (Massachusetts Institute of Technology, European Research Consortium for Informatics and Mathematics, Keio University, Beihang University). All Rights Reserved. This work is distributed under the W3C (http://www.w3.org/Consortium/Legal/copyright-software) in the hope that it will be useful, but WITHOUT ANY WARRANTY; without even the implied warranty of MERCHANTABILITY or FITNESS FOR A PARTICULAR PURPOSE.

* * *

Copyright Notice for Image 20 titled "Hyperledger Fabric Private Chaincode architecture":

This work is being provided by the copyright holders under the following license.

LICENSE

By obtaining and/or copying this work, you (the licensee) agree that you have read, understood, and will comply with the following terms and conditions.

Permission to copy, modify, and distribute this work, with or without modification, for any purpose and without fee or royalty is hereby granted, provided that you include the following on ALL copies of the work or portions thereof, including modifications:

- The full text of this NOTICE in a location viewable to users of the redistributed or derivative work.

- Any pre-existing intellectual property disclaimers, notices, or terms and conditions. If none exist, the W3C Software and Document Short Notice should be included.

- Notice of any changes or modifications, through a copyright statement on the new code or document such as "This software or document includes material copied from or derived from [title and URI of the W3C document]. Copyright © [YEAR] W3C® (MIT, ERCIM, Keio, Beihang)."

DISCLAIMERS

* * *

* * *

http://www.apache.org/licenses/

TERMS AND CONDITIONS FOR USE, REPRODUCTION, AND DISTRIBUTION

1. Definitions.

"License" shall mean the terms and conditions for use, reproduction, and distribution as defined by Sections 1 through 9 of this document.

"Licensor" shall mean the copyright owner or entity authorized by the copyright owner that is granting the License.

"Legal Entity" shall mean the union of the acting entity and all other entities that control, are controlled by, or are under common control with that entity. For the purposes of this definition, **"control"** means (i) the power, direct or indirect, to cause the direction or management of such entity, whether by contract or otherwise, or (ii) ownership of fifty percent (50%) or more of the outstanding shares, or (iii) beneficial ownership of such entity.

"You" (or **"Your"**) shall mean an individual or Legal Entity exercising permissions granted by this License.

"Source" form shall mean the preferred form for making modifications, including but not limited to software source code, documentation source, and configuration files.

"Object" form shall mean any form resulting from mechanical transformation or translation of a Source form, including but not limited to compiled object code, generated documentation, and conversions to other media types.

"Work" shall mean the work of authorship, whether in Source or Object form, made available under the License, as indicated by a copyright notice that is included in or attached to the work (an example is provided in the Appendix below).

"Derivative Works" shall mean any work, whether in Source or Object form, that is based on (or derived from) the Work and for which the editorial revisions, annotations, elaborations, or other modifications represent, as a whole, an original work of authorship. For the purposes of this License, Derivative Works shall not include works that remain separable from, or merely link (or bind by name) to the interfaces of, the Work and Derivative Works thereof.

"Contribution" shall mean any work of authorship, including the original version of the Work and any modifications or additions to that Work or Derivative Works thereof, that is intentionally submitted to Licensor for inclusion in the Work by the copyright owner or by an individual or Legal Entity authorized to submit on behalf of the copyright owner. For the purposes of this definition, **"submitted"** means any form of electronic, verbal, or written communication sent to the Licensor or its representatives, including but not limited to communication on electronic mailing lists, source code control systems, and issue tracking systems that are managed by, or on behalf of, the Licensor for the purpose of discussing and improving the Work, but excluding communication that is conspicuously marked or otherwise designated in writing by the copyright owner as **"Not a Contribution."**

"Contributor" shall mean Licensor and any individual or Legal Entity on behalf of whom a Contribution has been received by Licensor and subsequently incorporated within the Work.

2. Grant of Copyright License. Subject to the terms and conditions of this License, each Contributor hereby grants to You a perpetual, worldwide, non-exclusive, no-charge, royalty-free, irrevocable copyright license to reproduce, prepare Derivative Works of, publicly display, publicly perform, sublicense, and distribute the Work and such Derivative Works in Source or Object form.

3. Grant of Patent License. Subject to the terms and conditions of this License, each Contributor hereby grants to You a perpetual, worldwide, non-exclusive, no-charge, royalty-free, irrevocable (except as stated in this section) patent license to make, have made, use, offer to sell, sell, import, and otherwise transfer the Work, where such license applies only to those patent claims licensable by such Contributor that are necessarily infringed by their Contribution(s) alone or by combination of their Contribution(s) with the Work to which such Contribution(s) was submitted. If You institute patent litigation against any entity (including a cross-claim or counterclaim in a lawsuit) alleging that the Work or a Contribution incorporated within the Work constitutes direct or contributory patent infringement, then any patent licenses granted to You under this License for that Work shall terminate as of the date such litigation is filed.

4. Redistribution. You may reproduce and distribute copies of the Work or Derivative Works thereof in any medium, with or without modifications, and in Source or Object form, provided that You meet the following conditions:

1. You must give any other recipients of the Work or Derivative Works a copy of this License; and

2. You must cause any modified files to carry prominent notices stating that You changed the files; and

3. You must retain, in the Source form of any Derivative Works that You distribute, all copyright, patent, trademark, and attribution notices from the Source form of the Work, excluding those notices that do not pertain to any part of the Derivative Works; and

4. If the Work includes a **"NOTICE"** text file as part of its distribution, then any Derivative Works that You distribute must include a readable copy of the attribution notices contained within such NOTICE file, excluding those notices that do not pertain to any part of the Derivative Works, in at least one of the following places: within a NOTICE text file distributed as part of the Derivative Works; within the Source form or documentation, if provided along with the Derivative Works; or, within a display generated by the Derivative Works, if and wherever such third-party notices normally appear. The contents of the NOTICE file are for informational purposes only and do not modify the License. You may add Your own attribution notices within Derivative Works that You distribute, alongside or as an addendum to the NOTICE text from the Work, provided that such additional attribution notices cannot be construed as modifying the License.

You may add Your own copyright statement to Your modifications and may provide additional or different license terms and conditions for use, reproduction, or distribution of Your modifications, or for any such Derivative Works as a whole, provided Your use, reproduction, and distribution of the Work otherwise complies with the conditions stated in this License.

5. Submission of Contributions. Unless You explicitly state otherwise, any Contribution intentionally submitted for inclusion in the Work by You to the

Licensor shall be under the terms and conditions of this License, without any additional terms or conditions. Notwithstanding the above, nothing herein shall supersede or modify the terms of any separate license agreement you may have executed with Licensor regarding such Contributions.

6. Trademarks. This License does not grant permission to use the trade names, trademarks, service marks, or product names of the Licensor, except as required for reasonable and customary use in describing the origin of the Work and reproducing the content of the NOTICE file.

7. Disclaimer of Warranty. Unless required by applicable law or agreed to in writing, Licensor provides the Work (and each Contributor provides its Contributions) on an "AS IS" BASIS, WITHOUT WARRANTIES OR CONDITIONS OF ANY KIND, either express or implied, including, without limitation, any warranties or conditions of TITLE, NON-INFRINGEMENT, MERCHANTABILITY, or FITNESS FOR A PARTICULAR PURPOSE. You are solely responsible for determining the appropriateness of using or redistributing the Work and assume any risks associated with Your exercise of permissions under this License.

8. Limitation of Liability. In no event and under no legal theory, whether in tort (including negligence), contract, or otherwise, unless required by applicable law (such as deliberate and grossly negligent acts) or agreed to in writing, shall any Contributor be liable to You for damages, including any direct, indirect, special, incidental, or consequential damages of any character arising as a result of this License or out of the use or inability to use the Work (including but not limited to damages for loss of goodwill, work stoppage, computer failure or malfunction, or any and all other commercial damages or losses), even if such Contributor has been advised of the possibility of such damages.

9. Accepting Warranty or Additional Liability. While redistributing the Work or Derivative Works thereof, You may choose to offer, and charge a fee for, acceptance of support, warranty, indemnity, or other liability obligations and/or rights consistent with this License. However, in accepting such obligations, You may act only on Your own behalf and on Your sole responsibility, not on behalf of any other Contributor, and only if You agree to indemnify, defend, and hold each Contributor harmless for any liability incurred by, or claims asserted against, such Contributor by reason of your accepting any such warranty or additional liability.

END OF TERMS AND CONDITIONS

* * *

Hyperledger Avalon Architecture Overview
(https://github.com/hyperledger/avalon/tree/main/docs/)

Hyperledger Foundation, Licensed under CC BY 4.0
(https://creativecommons.org/licenses/by/4.0/)

*9 7 8 1 5 4 4 5 3 3 8 2 7 *